music and the ineffable

PRINCETON UNIVERSITY PRESS

Princeton and Oxford

music and the ineffable

Vladimir Jankélévitch

Translated by Carolyn Abbate

© Éditions du Seuil, Paris, 1983. The first edition of this work was published in France under the title *La Musique et l'Ineffable* in 1961 by Éditions Armand Colin

English translation © 2003 by Princeton University Press

Published by Princeton University Press, 41 William Street, Princeton, New Jersey 08540
In the United Kingdom: Princeton University Press, 3 Market Place, Woodstock, Oxfordshire OX20 1SY

LIBRARY OF CONGRESS CATALOGING-IN-PUBLICATION DATA
Jankélévitch, Vladimir.
[Musique et l'ineffable. English]
Music and the ineffable / Vladimir Jankélévitch ;
translated by Carolyn Abbate.
p.   cm.
Includes bibliographical references and index.
ISBN 0-691-09047-5 (cloth : alk. paper)
1. Music—Philosophy and aesthetics.   I. Abbate, Carolyn.   II. Title.
ML3800 .J242 2003
781.1'7—dc21   2002069299

British Library Cataloging-in-Publication Data is available

This book is published with the cooperation of the French Ministry of Culture–Centre national du livre

This book has been composed in Minion and Viant

Printed on acid-free paper. ∞

www.pupress.princeton.edu

Printed in the United States of America

3   5   7   9   10   8   6   4   2

ISBN-13: 978-0-691-09047-4 (cloth)

Contents

The *Charme* of Jankélévitch

ARNOLD I. DAVIDSON

No philosopher of this century has ever written on music with more power, more passionately and more persuasively, than Vladimir Jankélévitch.[1] His books and essays make us re-hear twentieth-century music in its entirety, above all in light of his descriptions of an aesthetics and morality of simplicity in which the virtue of understatement is made to stand out against the excesses of magniloquence: "The arid and sparing concision of a Ravel, the austerity of a Falla, the heroic held-back quality of a Debussy: these are lessons in reticence and sobriety for those suffering from affective exhibitionism and musical incontinence."[2] Nowhere are these virtues more pure than in the piano music of the great Catalan composer Federico Mompou, to whom Jankélévitch dedicated a brilliant chapter of his book *La présence lointaine.* Above all, in Mompou's *Musica callada*, in pieces that often last less than two minutes, the moral force and the aesthetic power of this simplicity are made present to the ear. As Jankélévitch described it, "All of the effort of catharsis consists in cutting away the inessential, that is to say in trimming the flowers of rhetoric, and in reducing the buzzing of discourse to its most simple expression . . . sobriety, decency, under-

statement: these are other names for the virtue of renuncia-
tion."[3]

Mompou well understood the difference between the exoteric brevity and the esoteric greatness of his piano pieces, a
perception that explains his confession that the word *piecette*
disturbed him when used to characterize his works: "This de-
stroys everything essential to my concision, which constitutes
the greatness of my work, and of its aesthetic sentiment."[4] The
greatness of concision is here played against the grandiosity of
inflation. What Jankélévitch wrote about Manuel de Falla
could be said not only of Mompou but of all the composers
that constitute Jankélévitch's school of *askesis.* "It goes immediately to the essential, and it says only that which must be
said, without cunning, without overburdening, scorning the
ogres of excess and inflation. There is no place in this work
either for the *diplodocus* that is *Siegfried,* or for the hags of
Walküre."[5] And no one has been better able to draw from this
music a lesson that is simultaneously aesthetic, moral, and
metaphysical:

> Understatement (which is not taken in by [excess]) is
> thus the opposite of emphasis, just as seriousness is the
> opposite of futility. God, according to scripture, does not
> come with the noise of wrathfulness, but as impercepti-
> bly as a breeze. Or (not according to scripture, but as I
> prefer to put it, to evoke *Pelléas et Mélisande* one more
> time): God arrives on tiptoe, furtively, pianissimo, just
> like Death in act 5: an almost-nothing, an imperceptible
> sigh.[6]

Jankélévitch always appreciated the transcendence of virtuosity—this is evident in his extraordinary book *Liszt et la
rhapsodie. Essai sur la virtuosité*—but was a tireless critic of
exhibitionism. And even if he sided with simplicity, he fought
against the threat of complacency. A self-satisfied innocence is
a false innocence; therefore Jankélévitch constantly unmasked

the sometimes imperceptible difference between the authentic

and the "simile": "The difference between modesty and vanity
is caught by the naked eye. But to distinguish false modesty
from true modesty, bad faith from good faith, more or less
hypocritical sincerity from sincere sincerity, requires as much
subtlety and intuition as it does to distinguish between seriousness and humor."[7]

In speaking of music, Jankélévitch gave a name to that particular spiritual difference that separates forms of perfection
inspiring "only boredom and indifference" in us from movements accomplished by poetic grace: *charme,* the Charm or
the summons made by the work of art.[8] As he writes, "Of
course, it is easy to note the decorative, distinctive marks that
are supposedly characteristic of Fauré's language. But someone who enumerates the marks has still said nothing. Someone who knows all the marks knows nothing if he or she does
not know the exact *manner* and occasion."[9] That which escapes any such enumeration is the *charme* of Fauré, the Fauréian manner. Jankélévitch, with his absolute mastery of musical technique, never turned his back on the necessity of
aesthetic intuition:

> Technical analysis is a means of refusing to abandon
> oneself spontaneously to grace, and abandonment is the
> request that the Charm makes of us. The phobia about
> consent, the fear of appearing bewitched, the coquetry
> of refusal, the resolve not to "submit," are the social and
> sociological forms assumed by alienation, just as the
> spirit of contradiction is a form of mimicry. Maniac an-
> tihedonism is the mark of the technician, and is akin in
> its frivolity to a love for Viennese waltzes.[10]

There are no technical recipes for the production of *charme,*
for generating the simple power of "the innocent transactions
of the Charm; the Charm that is graceful, without complacency, knowing no changes of heart or mind, no backtrack-

ings upon reflection; it is [an] efferent, transformational force."[11] As something that can convert us, this *charme* is able to make "every listener into a poet."[12] In his book *Le je-en-sais-quoi et le presque-rien*, Jankélévitch gives this splendid description of *Charme*:

> *Charme is* what makes sure that tedious perfections will not be left as a *dead letter*: when awakened, activated, animated, dead perfections become capable of arousing love, and only then are they alive. . . . In opposition to every definite thing (*res*), is *charme* not the very operation of beauty, the *poetic* influx through which beauty—far from remaining exposed, passive and quiescent, like a wax statue under the gaze of the spectator—will enter in a transitive relation with the human? . . . *Charme* makes beauty not only *actual* but *efficatious*. (Plotinus) had a term to indicate inefficatious beauty, perfection that does not act, and that is literally as "perfect" as the passive past participle. He called it [. . .] *lazy beauty*.[13]

For Jankélévitch, the true virtues of simplicity, of sincerity, of innocence, are incompatible with idleness.

Not by chance did Jankélévitch speak of *charme* in the same way that he spoke of love when he described our moral life: "Without the general idea of love, without the enlivening idea of living charity, the detail of the prescriptions is nothing but a *dead letter*."[14] In Jankélévitch's moral philosophy, love is never an idle thing; like *charme*, it is an operation, a movement, a transitive relation: "Goodness is nothing if it is not charity . . . greatness is nothing if it does not magnify smallness, if it is not literally magnificent . . . purity is impure if it is not purifying. And conversely, a goodness that improves nothing, a quiescent and idle goodness, is like a flame that does not shine, it does not illuminate anybody, it does not warm anything: this inactive goodness contradicts itself."[15]

Moreover, just as forms of musical "perfection" that apparently lack nothing lack everything when they do not possess
charme, so an impeccable "virtue" without love lacks nothing
but the essential: "It lacks nothing and yet lacks something.
. . . It lacks something without which 'virtues' would be only
that which they are: brilliant *performance* and clanging cym-
bal. It lacks the charitable intention, or the accent of sincerity
and of spontaneous conviction. No one can be mistaken
about this: it lacks a soul. Everything is present, except the
heart, which is not there; therefore nothing is there."[16] The
distance between a "heartfelt charity" and a brilliant execution
of "virtue" is parallel to the dissonance between *charme* and
bluff.[17]

The musical powers of *charme* and the moral powers of
love are thematically united in Fauré's *Pénélope* and in Falla's
El amor brujo. Pénélope exclaims, "Nous allons vivre . . .
vivre!"[18] Here is the love that in the final scene of *El amor
brujo* exclaims, "Cantad, campanas, cantad!" Thus we are
granted the insight that "the enchanted soul is not a bewitched soul, but an enamored soul."[19] "Doubtless *El amor
brujo* begins, like *Tristan*, with black magic and the love potion that leads nowhere; but while the Tristanesque witchcraft
finds its resolution only in death, the monsters of *El amor
brujo* vanish with the dawn and the morning dew, the *angelus*
of dawn and hope."[20]

This joyful love is not the love without effort of a supernatural being but the victorious love of a finite creature, that
is to say a creature tested by tribulations, whose love can be
continuously threatened, a creature whose height or depth is
never attained without *activity*. Sharing "the essentially unstable character of virtue, and the continuous re-creation, the
dynamism of effort that this precariousness imposes on us,"
Candelas's love in *El Amor brujo* incorporates an untiring
struggle, while it expresses an infinite glory.[21] To give voice at

the same time to both, like Ginesa Ortega in her recording of *El amor brujo*, makes us remember our need for redeeming human love, and it reveals to us the possibility, a possibility always open, of this love.[22] And we already know that this love, which possesses the power of *charme*, is transformational: "The unknowable something engendered by love-sickness becomes joyous fervor and freedom savored in full daylight, the unknowable something that is divine. The Charm succeeds black magic, and the ineffable the unsayable. Among all the philosophical and alchemical transmutations that make metamorphosis possible, none is more miraculous than the transfiguration of an inspired heart: 'sing, bells; sing, joy; my love draws near'."[23]

When one reads Jankélévitch on music, and especially when one reads *Music and the Ineffable*, one is always compelled to ask—even in the case of his stupendous books—what meaning the aesthetics of music might have for philosophy in general. Almost no one has grasped the link, very subtle but also very profound in Jankélévitch's writings, between *charme* as it is engendered by music and love toward another person.[24] Without the one, without the other, we are dead, not dead like the dead, but dead like the living.[25]

Jankélévitch's Singularity

CAROLYN ABBATE

Music is no cipher; it is not awaiting the decoder.
Musical works do not express emotion or reflect optical phenomena, nor do they tell stories, nor represent ideologies unless such works are degraded a priori, already propaganda, in
which case they are no longer music. Music has a power over
our bodies and minds wildly disproportionate to its lack of
obvious or concrete meaning, as to its slippery aesthetic status. Nonetheless, music in general, musical devices and processes, and specific musical works in particular, are always
bound to the "world down here below," to a human experience of time, to human bodies and human spirituality, to culture and the past. Musical sound is both absolutely, crudely
material, and *cosa mentale*, a thing of the mind, altered in
innumerable ways by human intentionality. And if there is
empty, incontinent music (German music falls into this category), there is other music that enchants in a disenchanted
world: heroically held-back music, the music of reticence and
verve.

Music and the Ineffable asks us to imagine metaphors and
analogies that "explain" music only to dismiss them; to realize
that it is in imagining and dismissing, and doing it again, and

again, that one asymptotically approaches an intimation of something that will elude any and all searchlights. We are enjoined to embrace aporia as a form of fertility and gnostic futility as a form of grace, a reminder about humility, in a book whose intellectual fireworks are only one of its explosive charges. Like much of Vladimir Jankélévitch's writing, *Music and the Ineffable*, first published in 1961, upends complacencies hard won through years of disciplinary servitude. Jankélévitch was a central figure in French intellectual life, and with Adorno and Bloch, one of the twentieth century's great philosophers of music, yet he is all but unknown in Anglo-American philosophy, criticism, or musicology. I first encountered his writings more than a decade ago through his Ravel book, originally published in 1939 and reissued in 1956. It was translated into English in 1959 (the trade-book publisher, apparently, imagined it a general life-and-works text), and I found a copy of this translation at a used book shop.[1] I still remember the astonishment I felt as I read it: Music was present in ways that instantly seemed both unprecedented and true, the imagination given expression in the book was completely unbound, there was such virtuoso command of so many things—all this was quite unusual in musicological writing. What was extraordinary as well was the attention Jankélévitch paid to such concepts as gentleness, violence, reserve, and caritas, to human subjects' sense of self in relation to others, all in terms of Ravel's music. Who was this man?

That was my question, and for Anglo-American readers it still needs to be asked and addressed. Vladimir Jankélévitch (1903–85) was born in Bourges and belonged to a family of Russian-Jewish emigrés who were naturalized French citizens. His father, Samuel Jankélévitch, was Freud's French translator and translated numerous other philosophical and religious texts from several languages, including standard works of Hegel and Schelling. Vladimir Jankélévitch studied Russian literature at the École des langues orientales and philosophy at the École normale superieure in the 1920s; in 1924, he published an important article on Henri Bergson, whose influence on Jankélévitch was profound. His thesis on Schelling appeared in print in 1932; he submitted a supplementary thesis on ethics as well, and in 1931 wrote a book that still stands as a major text on Bergson's work.[2] He taught philosophy at the Institut français de Prague (1927–33) and, after his return to France in 1933, at various institutions, notably the universities at Lyon and Lille. His musical life accompanied this philosophical life from the outset. A gifted amateur pianist, he was close to Gabriel Fauré's sons and had ties to the Satie disciples known as "les Six"; his sister, the pianist Ida Jankélévitch, was part of their circle.[3] By the late 1930s he had completed two books on music, the Ravel book and one on Fauré, as well as several articles.[4]

For French intellectuals, what happened next became a legend of heroism cited as often as possible, that it might erase a general sense of collective shame. Jankélévitch was mobilized to fight in the war in 1939 and was wounded in 1940. After the Nazi invasion, his citizenship, like that of all naturalized French Jews, was revoked; he fled to Toulouse where he taught at the university and joined the Résistance, writing for one of the most important anti-Nazi organizations in Vichy France, the Mouvement national contre le racisme. At the same time—with the help of former students in Lyon—he managed to publish several works on music and philosophy, including an extraordinary essay centered on Chopin, Le Nocturne.[5] He reemerged into normal academic life after the war, and in 1951 was appointed to the chair in moral philosophy at the Sorbonne, which he held until his retirement in 1978. During the 1950s, '60s, and '70s, he wrote extensively on ethics and musical aesthetics.

For readers outside France, three points of reference, three names, will serve both to invoke a milieu and to suggest his influence: His voice, like his philosophy, "left an indelible mark" on Emmanuel Levinas; he played piano duets with Roland Barthes; he was mentor to Catherine Clément, and his musical aesthetics shaped her thinking in several domains.[6] Barthes's debt to Jankélévitch's philosophy of music is profound and seldom recognized among Barthes's Anglo-American admirers. To cite only one example, Barthes's essay "Musica Practica,"[7] with its emphasis on music as something done by the body, seems almost to flow directly from the aesthetics systematically articulated in *Music and the Ineffable*, from Jankélévitch's insistence that "making is of an entirely different order from saying. Composing music; playing it and singing it; or even hearing it in recreating it—are these not three modes of doing, three attitudes that are drastic not gnostic, not of the hermeneutic order of knowledge?" Or, "Music has this in common with poetry, and love, and even with duty: music is not made to be spoken of, but for one to *do*: it is not made to be said, but to be 'played'."[8]

That Jankélévitch has not been translated when his philosophical colleagues—Derrida, Foucault, Merleau-Ponty, Clément, and Levinas—were made accessible to English-speaking readers long ago is perhaps due to two unrelated circumstances. First is the force and strangeness of his language, his way of writing French, seeming always breathless, using litany and repetition to disrupt regular rhythm and conventions of thought, unconcerned with normal scholarly discourse or fashion, never abstruse but very hard to capture. His writing is a reproach to academic prose in every language, to torpor, prolixity, and ugliness at one extreme, to frivolity and vanity at the other: it brings our failures home to us. Thus, aside from the Ravel book, very little has appeared in English,[9] although in 1996 his most controversial essay—"Should We Pardon Them?" (1971)—was translated by Ann Hobart.[10] The second explanation for Jankélévitch's "difficulty" shouts from the pages of that essay, which is emotionally, ethically wrenching, as Arnold Davidson puts it, "one of the most morally

powerful texts ever written about Nazi atrocities, a p
contribution, the equal of unequalled works like Prin
The Drowned and the Saved."[11] Jankélévitch never for
Germans and could not return to their art, their phi
or their music. His colleagues made their peace with G ....,
and re-embraced its intellectual traditions, burnishing their
reputations in embroidering upon those traditions for a new
generation. Jankélévitch seldom spoke the names again and
then almost exclusively with a certain scorn.

This refusal put him at odds with the fashionable compro-
mises of post-war academic convention. Yet, in terms of his
writing on music, it is only one aspect of a book that still seems
radical forty years later. So much of what he says disturbs the
comfortable state of musicology (old and new alike) that it is
hard to know how to begin to signal, in advance, where the
tremors might be felt. For one thing, music for Jankélévitch is a
French and Russo-Slavic phenomenon, with Spain in secondary orbit. It is as if German music simply does not exist except
as trivial and marginal (and the composer who invented Love
Potions and Flower Maidens is rarely named). In his account of
modernism, Fauré, Debussy, Satie, and Ravel are seen as reject-
ing expressionism and consequently embracing various alternatives to loquaciousness—objective impression, inexpressiveness and automatism, violence, mask—which become the
paradoxical, esoteric signs of concealed passion. This aesthetic
genealogy of modernism, however, is bound up with recurring
questions about the metaphysics and ontology of music, in
which Jankélévitch flies his Bergsonian colors high, by insisting
that music is a material phenomenon in time. Seeing musical
works as temporal, as a form of Becoming, means that they are
not structures. Jankélévitch dismantles the claims of musical
semantics and exposes the suspect metaphysical urge that un-
derlies musical hermeneutics, leading him to the conclusion
that musical works are not an argument; they cannot be "followed" except by false analogy.

Music is, as he says, "drastic," not "gnostic": works are made, brought into being by labor, and it is in the irreversible experience of playing them or listening to them that the "meaning of their meaning" is given voice. Attempts to ascribe limited, specific social or symbolic meanings to music in retrospect represent—though only at their worst—a morose refusal to accept one's existence in time and a manifestation of anxiety: of the desire *not* to be transmuted or transported by what Jankélévitch (following mystic philosopher Henri Bremond) calls *charme*. This word is difficult to translate because *charme* suggests an almost audible quality, a sound that comes into being and produces effects. But one must discard whatever implications either of hypnosis or niceness the word Charm may have in English, since *charme*—the summons made by enchantment—is an aesthetic phenomenon to which we react not passively but actively, by being changed, changing ourselves. Enchantment—the state engendered by Charm—is a state of continence and, often, of delight, at an opposite pole to bewitchment (*envoutement*) in which one is involuntarily transfixed and spiritually immobilized by "black magic" (*sortilèges*). The experience of this "Charm," the ways that one is transformed in response to it, is equivalent to the power of love, caritas and eros—the love of another or for an Other—in Jankélévitch's moral philosophy.[12]

Music and the Ineffable thus concentrates our attention on the intense materiality of music: on the hands and throats of the musicians, on performance as a half-hour of extreme peril, living noise amid a general condition of silence; or simply as visceral, physical work. Jankélévitch notes that we imagine ourselves as a detached and sovereign consciousness with music as a passive medium at our disposal—in which to express ourselves, to compose with, to play and interpret, or to assign meanings to, as we see fit—but rejects this as mistaken: We are as much music's tool as we are the worker who uses it.

For instance, the resistance and particularity of musical objects (like instruments) leads us in directions we could not have anticipated. And thus we will lunge, finding our way through time, which does not let us stop to re-do what was done. This concept of improvisation—an alliance between courage and humility in the process of "doing"—is important to Jankélévitch's ideas about moral action. In his writings on Liszt, he sets the spiritual automaton, who acts like a mechanism, playing strictly according to graphic prescriptions, against the improvisational being, who goes to places where the notes might lead without (at the time) knowing where.

No précis can describe *Music and the Ineffable.* One must experience it as a whole, concrete and specific, enjoy the special shock of an observation that music is the least erotic of all the arts,[13] in a book that unravels the philosophical grudge against music (from Plato to Nietzsche) while lingering over impossible performance instructions in piano pieces by Debussy and wondering what hand, made of which unknown element, could realize them in the world. My hope is that this English version conveys not only conceptual flashpoints that are important in Jankélévitch's philosophy, but as much as possible—and this is equally significant, as he himself would have pointed out—the rhythms and cadences, the almost physically present energy, the passion, and the paradox of perpetual newness that characterizes his unique voice.

In conclusion, I want to acknowledge the many individuals who helped bring this translation to fruition. Madame Lucienne Jankélévitch gave her permission for *La musique et l'ineffable* to appear in English, and Françoise Schwab, Jankélévitch's literary executor, blessed the idea with her approval. Fred Appel and Walter Lippincott at Princeton University Press lent their critical support to the project. Scott Paulin, Eli Friedlander, Sindhu Revuluri, Jason Stell, and Michal Grover-Friedlander were fellow participants in a seminar that dealt with Jankélévitch's oeuvre; their aplomb continually amazed me. David Powell rescued me from certain Francophone oubliettes; James Woolard transcribed Jankélévitch's flights of ancient Greek for me, as well as translating them and / or locating their sources and generally bringing them back down to earth. Above all, however, I want to thank Arnold Davidson. When I first announced that I wanted to translate *La musique et l'ineffable* I sensed stunned disbelief, but it lasted only an instant, to be succeeded by unflagging enthusiasm, numerous practical interventions, moral support, subtle badgering (only when needed), and a stream of invaluable information and advice. Without him, and his conviction that Jankélévitch's work *must* become known to as wide an audience as possible, this translation would never have come into being.

Preface

MUSIC AND THE INEFFABLE

[handwritten: hope for thing but impossible to achieve]

"What is music?" Gabriel Fauré asks himself, seeking the "untranslatable point," an unreal chimera, one that raises us "above that which is."[1] This is the period when Fauré drafts the second movement of his first quintet, and still: he has no idea what music is, or even if it is *something*. With music, a twofold complication will engender both metaphysical and moral problems, and nourishes our sense of perplexity. On the one hand, music is at once expressive and inexpressive, serious and frivolous, deep and superficial; music has a meaning and does not have a meaning. Is music mere divertissement, without import? Or is it an enciphered language, the hieroglyph that is the sign of a mystery? Or perhaps both, together? But this essential equivocation has a moral aspect as well: there is a puzzling contrast, an ironic, scandalous disproportion between the incantatory power of music, and the fundamental inevidence of musical beauty. *[handwritten: magic spell charm]*

At times, the sublime shattering evident-ness of such beauty, in the *Psalm XII* of Liszt, the Symphony in F Major op. 76 of Dvořák, Fauré's second quartet, *Parfums de la Nuit, The Legend of the Invisible City of Kitezh, Boris Godunov,* seems to end all equivocation once and for all. But the mocking contradiction

[handwritten: ambiguous language in effort to conceal]

[handwritten: all different forms of beauty]

between music's power and music's ambiguity will be reborn, unable to be resolved. Is the Charm engendered by music a form of deception or a principle of wisdom? We will consider whether the letter of these contradictions is not precisely to be found in the inscrutable workings of the musical Charm and in the innocence of a poetic act that has time as its only dimension.

did he mean latter?

enigmatic/mysterious/incomprehensible

etymology
poesis = creative

"we hold this truth to be self-evident"
no so for music

THE "ETHICS" AND
THE "METAPHYSICS" OF MUSIC

Music acts upon human beings, on their nervous
systems and their vital processes: in 1849 Liszt wrote a song,
"Die Macht der Musik" to a text by the Duchess Helène d'Or-
léans: music paying tribute to its own capacities. This power—
which poems and colors possess occasionally and indirectly—
is in the case of music particularly immediate, drastic, and
indiscreet: "it penetrates to the center of the soul," Plato says,
"and gains possession of the soul in the most energetic fashion," καταδύεται εἰς τὸ ἐντὸς τῆς ψυχῆς ὅ τε ῥυθμὸς καὶ
ἁρμονία, καὶ ἐρρωμενέστατα ἅπτεται αὐτῆς.[1] Schopenhauer,
on this point, echoes Plato. By means of massive irruptions,
music takes up residence in our intimate self and seemingly
elects to make its home there. The man inhabited and pos-
sessed by this intruder, the man robbed of a self, is no longer
himself: he has become nothing more than a vibrating string,
a sounding pipe. He trembles madly under the bow or the
fingers of the instrumentalist; and just as Apollo fills the Py-
thia's lungs, so the organ's powerful voice and the harp's gentle accents take possession of the listener. This process, at once
irrational and shameful, takes place on the margins of truth,
and thus borders more on magic than on empirical science.

Something that wants to persuade us with singing, rather ¦an convince us with reason, implements an art of pleasing ...at addresses the passions, that is, one that subjugates in suggesting and that enslaves the listener through the fraudulent and charlatan power of melody, weakens him through harmonic glamour or the fascinations of rhythm. To accomplish this, the process does not tap the logistical or governing aspects of the mind but rather engages the mind's entire psychosomatic element. If mathematical discourse is thinking that wishes to make itself comprehensible to other thought by becoming transparent to it, a harmonic modulation is an *act* that expects to influence a *being*, and by "influence" one must also understand a clandestine causality, just as in astrology or sorcery: illegal maneuvers, black arts. Solon the lawmaker is a sage, but Orpheus the enchanter is a magician. A vocalization is not an excuse and a perfume is not an argument.

Thus, when a human being reaches the age of reason, he struggles against this unseemly and illegal seizure of his person, not wanting to give in to enchantment, that is, to go where the songs are leading. The magical induction becomes a seduction and thus trickery, and an adult refuses to be captivated, resisting the beliefs suggested to him by the auletic. A woman who persuades solely by means of her presence and its perfumes, that is, by the magical exhalations of her being, the night that envelops us, music, which secures our allegiance solely through the Charm engendered by a trill or an arpeggio, will therefore be the object of a deep suspicion. Being bewitched is not worthy of a rational person. Just as a masculine Will insists that its decisions are made on concrete grounds—and will never admit a preference founded in emotion—so masculine Reason will never admit itself prone to seduction. What is science for if not to sustain us against the intoxications of night and the temptations exercised by the enchantress appearance?

Music, the sonorous phantasm, is the most futile of mere

appearances, and appearance, which with neither the force to probe nor any intelligible determinism is nonetheless able to persuade the dazzled fool, is in some way the objectification of our weakness. A man who has sobered up, a demystified man, does not forgive himself for having once been the dupe of misleading powers; a man who is abstaining, having awakened from his nocturnal exhilaration, blushes for having given in to dark causality. Once morning has returned, he disowns the pleasurable arts themselves, along with his own skills of pleasing. Strong and serious minds, prosaic and positive minds: maybe their prejudice with regard to music comes from sobering up. In the presence of the scabrous power unleashed by music, a number of attitudes are possible. We can distinguish three: the right of use and enjoyment, passionate resentment, and refusal pure and simple.

[handwritten margin notes: indecent; — enjoyment — resentment — refusal]

ORPHEUS OR THE SIRENS?

Plato thinks that the power to drive onlookers mad should not be left to any random flutist; that the musician, like the orator, plays with dangerous forms of enchantment; and that the state should regulate the use of musical influences and contain them within a framework of sound medicine. That which is "musical," however, is not the voice of the Sirens but rather Orpheus's songs. The mermaid sirens, enemies of the Muses, have only one goal: to reroute, mislead, and delay Odysseus. In other words, they derail the dialectic, the law of the itinerary that leads our mind toward duty and truth.

In Mikhaíl Lermontov's poem *The Demon*, perfidious Tamara's songs captivate the voyager and lead him astray on the path that leads to death. To avoid seduction, what can one do besides make oneself deaf to all melody and to suppress, along with temptation, sensation itself? In fact, the musicians who permit the sirens of oblivion and the Rusalkas to sing—Debussy, for example, or Balakirev, or Rimsky-Korsakov—are actually letting us hear the voice of Orpheus, because real music humanizes and civilizes. Music is not simply a captivating and fallacious ruse, subjugating without violence, capturing by captivating; it is also gentleness that makes gentle: in itself gentle, it makes those who hear it more gentle since music pacifies the monsters of instinct in all of us and tames passion's wild animals. Franz Liszt, in the preface to his symphonic poem *Orpheus*, shows us the "father of songs," ἀοιδᾶν πατήρ, as Pindar calls him, arresting the stones and charming ferocious beasts, making birds and waterfalls silent, bringing the supernatural benediction of art to nature itself: this, for Liszt, is the message of an Orphic civilization, as it was for the theosophist Fabre d'Olivet.[2]

Just as the dispatch rider in Plato's *Phaedo* tames a vicious warhorse to render it docile, εὐπειθής, so Orpheus harnesses lions to a plow that they might work the wasteland, and panthers to carriages that they might take families for their promenades; he channels wild torrents, and the torrents, becoming obedient, turn the wheels of the mills. All the creatures of creation assemble in a circle, attentive, around the orchestral conductor of lions; birds sound their arpeggios and waterfalls their murmurs. He who appeases the furious waves under the Argonauts' ship, who puts the redoubtable dragon of Colchide to sleep, who makes the animals and plants docile—even the inflexible Aides—he could well say, like Christ (who tamed another storm), πραός εἰμι, I am gentle. Inspired, the cantor does not tame the Cimmerian monsters by the whip but persuades them with his lyre; his proper weapon is not the bludgeon but a musical instrument. Michelet would no doubt say that the work of Orpheus completes the labors of Hercules, and that they are, both of them, heroes of culture and the supernatural: because just as the athlete colonizes and reclaims the desert by means of strength, the magician humanizes the inhuman by means of art's harmonious and melodious grace: the former exterminates evil, as much as the latter, architect-kitharist, coverts the evil into the human.

In his *Bible de l'humanité*, Michelet expounds in magnificent terms upon the battle of the lyre and the flute described in Aristotle's *Politics*: set against the Dionysian flute—the instrument chosen by the satyr Marsyas, the orgiastic flute of disgraceful intoxication—are Orpheus's phorminx and Apollo's kithara, arrayed in opposition. And just as the flute that tames rats and charms snakes is the suspect instrument, the languid, impudent instrument of the Thyrsian bearers, Orpheus antibarbarian constitutes the civilization of the lyre incarnate. This is the truly Apollonian lyre: an opera by Albert Roussel tells of its birth; Stravinsky consecrated *Apollon Musagète* to the god of light, leader of the Muses; Fauré set a *Hymne à Apollon* to music in honor of the god who transfixed the fearful dragon. The effeminate kitharist whom Kierkegaard denigrates in *Fear and Trembling*, citing the *Banquet*, is not a true Orpheus. Orpheus died victim to the Thracian Bacchantes, the drunken Maenads, that is to say, of the fury of passion, which tore him into pieces; as the enemy of the Bacchic god and the flutist god, Orpheus salutes the dawn and venerates Helios, the chaste and sober god of light. *Cave carmen*: beware of the Charm. But not at all: refuse, in general, to be swayed by a charm.

That, however, implies that one cannot distinguish between incantation and enchantment: there is abusive music, which, like rhetoric, is simple charlatanism and flatters the listener to enslave him, for the odes of Marsyas "bewitch" us as the discourse of Gorgias indoctrinates us. Yet there is also *melos* that does not give the lie to *logos*, and, as in Federico Mompou's album *Charmes* (1925), this melos has curing, appeasing, and exalting our being as its business: "To penetrate the soul," "To summon love," "To put suffering to rest," "To inspire joy" (so some of the titles). The music of the leader of the Muses exists

lodious grace: the former exterminates evil, as much as the latter, architect-kitharist, coverts the evil into the human.

In his *Bible de l'humanité*, Michelet expounds in magnificent terms upon the battle of the lyre and the flute described in Aristotle's *Politics*: set against the Dionysian flute—the instrument chosen by the satyr Marsyas, the orgiastic flute of disgraceful intoxication—are Orpheus's phorminx and Apollo's kithara, arrayed in opposition. And just as the flute that tames rats and charms snakes is the suspect instrument, the languid, impudent instrument of the Thyrsian bearers, Orpheus antibarbarian constitutes the civilization of the lyre incarnate. This is the truly Apollonian lyre: an opera by Albert Roussel tells of its birth; Stravinsky consecrated *Apollon Musagète* to the god of light, leader of the Muses; Fauré set a *Hymne à Apollon* to music in honor of the god who transfixed the fearful dragon. The effeminate kitharist whom Kierkegaard denigrates in *Fear and Trembling*, citing the *Banquet*, is not a true Orpheus. Orpheus died victim to the Thracian Bacchantes, the drunken Maenads, that is to say, of the fury of passion, which tore him into pieces; as the enemy of the Bacchic god and the flutist god, Orpheus salutes the dawn and venerates Helios, the chaste and sober god of light. *Cave carmen*: beware of the Charm. But not at all: refuse, in general, to be swayed by a charm.

That, however, implies that one cannot distinguish between incantation and enchantment: there is abusive music, which, like rhetoric, is simple charlatanism and flatters the listener to enslave him, for the odes of Marsyas "bewitch" us as the discourse of Gorgias indoctrinates us. Yet there is also *melos* that does not give the lie to *logos*, and, as in Federico Mompou's album *Charmes* (1925), this melos has curing, appeasing, and exalting our being as its business: "To penetrate the soul," "To summon love," "To put suffering to rest," "To inspire joy" (so some of the titles). The music of the leader of the Muses exists

The "Ethics" and the "Metaphysics" of Music

5

as a truth because it imposes the mathematical law of number—which is harmony—on the savage tumult of hunger, the law of measure—which is the beat—on the disorder of measureless chaos, and rhythmicized time, measured and stylized time, the time of corteges and ceremonies, on unequal time, time by turns languishing and convulsive, fastidious and precipitous: the time of our daily life. Alain, Stravinsky, Roland-Manuel: were they not agreed in recognizing that music is a kind of temporal metrics?

Music is suspect, to be sure, but it cannot be disavowed pure and simple. Preoccupied above all with moral education and with frugality, Plato rails only against the "Carian muse," the muse of those who weep and of effeminate sobs.[3] The third book of the *Republic* reserves all of its severity for the languid and pathetic modes, the Oriental modes, Ionian and Lydian, for their plaintive harmony, θρηνώδεις ἁρμονίαι.[4] Lamento and Appassionato: they are demoralizing. Indecent intoxication, μέθη, that alone, is capable of rendering the city's guardians feeble. It appears that the more "musical" music is—in the modern sense of the word—the less approbation it finds in Plato's thought. Musical, that is, in being melodic, in ascending and descending more freely through the scale. This is why the *Laws* condemns ἑτεροφωνία, heterophony, and the *Republic* πολυχορδία παναρμόνιος, polyharmonic multi-stringed instruments:[5] because instruments with many strings promote polyphonic complications and foster a taste for rhythmic variety and instrumental color. The flute's swift witticisms, the prestidigitation of the virtuoso, trills, vocalises, roulades, the tenor's fioratura, are, to be sure, related to an art of flattery that geometry slanders with the name Rhetoric. Plato reserves all his approbation for the least musical, least modulatory modes, the austere monody of the Dorian and the Phrygian, set in opposition to the honeyed Muse, γλυκεία μούση, her indubitable spells and her bewitching recitatives, who is too suave and too flattering to be truthful and who is

music's Function to state (Plato)
an ethical problem,

therefore more Siren than Muse. Plato appreciates the austere modes for their moral value, as much irenic as polemical: in war, they exalt courage, in peace, they serve well for prayers and hymns to the gods, and for the moral edification of youth.

In effect, such "music" is more a moral than a musical phenomenon, more didactic *teaching* than persuasive, and its function is in fact entirely objective. The beauty of custom, εὐηθεία (good character), conditions music's rhythmic and harmonic Charm, εὐαρμοστία (its well-composed quality) and εὐρυθμία (its graceful movement and order). The purpose of the severe Muse, the serious Muse, is to induce virtue and not enchant us by singing.

BEARING A GRUDGE AGAINST MUSIC

We shall therefore be impelled to disavow the "Carian Muse" (as she is called in the seventh book of the *Laws* and by Clement of Alexandria) but not because of pedagogical concerns, rather, by antimusical passion and by resentment. There is no doubt that Nietzsche continued to love what he disavowed, very much so: he is still secretly in love with the flower maidens who bewitched him. Like all renegades, the man who disavowed Wagner's romanticism, disavowed Schopenhauer's pessimism, and blasphemed even Socrates's moralism, nonetheless cannot bear to be parted from his own past and takes perverse pleasure in tormenting himself. Thus there is an aspect of passionate ambivalence, of amorous hatred and even masochism in Nietzsche's grudge against the musical eternal-feminine. For just as immorality is often simply excessive rigor on the rebound, an alibi produced to disguise a secret and passionate moral temperament, so melomania explains in certain cases the furious energy of melophobia.

This, at root, was the case with Tolstoy. Paul Boyer tells us how he was a rebel against the bewildering power of Chopin's fourth Ballade; Sergey Tolstoy confirms his father's extraordinary sensitivity to Romantic music. True, Tolstoy's grudge is that of a moralist, and Nietzsche's is that of an immoralist; in this, Tolstoy would be closer to Plato. Nonetheless, does Nietzsche not express himself as the sorely disappointed pedagogue, as the spokesman for a truly impossible virtue? The preface of *The Wanderer and His Shadow* (borrowing Plato's language almost literally)[6] speaks to us of the vague, ambiguous desires melting the iron of virile souls. Nietzsche finds such dangers in Tristan's magic potion, in the maddening brews that have made him drunk, in Romanticism's poisonous mushrooms, which spring up in the quagmires where fever and languor are lurking.

Perhaps Nietzsche has defined the distance that separates the particular trouble attributable to music from Socratic aporia: melos is troubling but not fertile, constituting neither a stimulating excess nor a gnostic perplexity. Rather, music is a sterile malaise that enervates and smothers conscience: as lullaby, putting it to sleep, as elegy, making it soft. Better still: in music in general Nietzsche sees the means of expression of nondialectical consciences and of apolitical peoples.[7] The former, in love with twilight dreams, with inexplicable thoughts and reverie, sink gratefully into the swamp of solitude; the latter, reduced to inaction and boredom by autocracy, take refuge in the inoffensive compensations and the consolations of music. Music, the decadent art, is the bad conscience of an introverted populace, which finds a substitute for their need to take civic action in works that are merely instrumental or vocal.

By contrast, Athenian democracy, being naturally sociable, abandons lyric black magic for gymnastic games, the palestra's battles, and the agora's debates. Athleticism, at the very least, entails the action of muscles, the real effort needed to move the obstacle or lift the object, by an expenditure of energy directly proportional to the weight of that object. Nietzsche no doubt wanted to say the following: music is not proper to dialogue, whose nature rests in exchange, the analysis of ideas, amicable collaboration that takes place mutually and equitably. Music does not allow the discursive, reciprocal communication of meaning but rather an immediate and ineffable communication; and this can only take place in the penumbra of melancholia, unilaterally, from hypnotist to the hypnotized.

It is hard to believe that Plato—the philosopher of the logos, of dialogue and dialectics—could avoid suspecting the trickery of tenor singing or the flutist's solo. This is also the essence of Tolstoy's prejudice. One day, when Goldenweiser had played Chopin for him, Lev Nikolayevich remarks: "wherever you want slaves, you need as much music as possible."[8] Lev Nikolayevich had confidence only in popular music. And as for Nietzsche, he famously saw in Bizet's music a means of detoxification, music able to restore joy, cleanliness, and virility to the mind. No longer with prosaic *gymnopédies* (as with Plato) but with acrobatic leaps and blinding light: that is how Nietzsche begins his purification cure, his sobering up, and his disillusionment. Without a doubt, Albeniz and Darius Milhaud would have trumpeted an even louder wake-up call and designed the most effective catharsis.

MUSIC AND ONTOLOGY

To grant music a moral function, however, it would seem necessary to amputate and discard all its pathos, everything heady and orgiastic in it, and, finally, to deprive oneself of poetic intoxication in any form. For music does not always convey the serenity of wise men: it fevers those who listen to it, drives them mad. Music is derationalizing and unhealthy. Thus in Tolstoy's famous moralizing novella (*The Kreutzer Sonata*, also not a little misogynistic) a musical work is accessory to an illicit passion. Proudhon himself, by inclination a serious, moral mind, accuses those who advocate the aesthetics of the game and "art for art's sake" of degeneracy. Alas, an

eagerness to resist temptation is no less suspect than temptation itself. The Puritan grudge against music, the persecution
of pleasure, hatred of seduction and spells, the antihedonist
obsession: in the end, all these are pathologies, just as mis-
ogyny is pathological.

Under such conditions, one is led to ask whether music
might not have a metaphysical significance rather than an ethical function. Throughout history, those human beings who
are fond of allegory have sought that which is signified by
music *beyond* the sound phenomenon, ἁρμονίη ἀφανὴς φα-
νερῆς κρείττων (the invisible harmony is more powerful than
the visible).[9] For there is an invisible and inaudible harmony,
suprasensible and supra-audible, and this is the true "key to
song." For Clement of Alexandria and Saint Augustine, for
the English mystic Richard Rolle, any singing perceptible to
the ears and the body is the exoteric envelope of a smooth,
ineffable, and celestial melody. Plotinus says that music perceptible to the senses is created by music anterior to sensible
perception. Music is of another realm. Harmony, if we believe
Fabre d'Olivet, resides neither in the instrument nor in physical phenomena (it is worth recalling that Fabre d'Olivet was
interested in Pythagorean arithmology, the Hebrew language,
and a kind of "musicosophy," a philosophical music that
would transmute souls). Richard Rolle and Antoine de Rojas
heard angel music: no doubt, our orchestral concerts are mere
pale understudies to such celestial concerts.

For Rimsky-Korsakov, the invisible city, Celestial Kitezh, reveals the esoteric sense of Lesser Kitezh. And nonetheless, the
carillons and jubilant canticles that resound in invisible Kitezh
vibrate materially as well, for terrestrial human beings. The
city is invisible. But its sublime music is not inaudible, because Rimsky-Korsakov, after all, is a musician and not a Neo-
platonic mystic.

It is the metaphysician, and not the musician, who dispar-
ages actual physical harmony for the sake of transcendent

paradigms and supernatural music. If Roland-Manuel (himself a musician) thinks that music "echoes of the order of the world," he nonetheless believes in music's autonomy. To decipher who-knows-what cryptic message as perceptible, to place a stethoscope on a canticle and hear something else in it and behind it, to perceive an allusion to something else in every song, to interpret that which is heard as the allegory of a secret, incredible meaning: these are the indelible traits of all hermeneutics, and are first and foremost applied in the interpretation of language. Anyone who reads between the lines or believes himself to have gotten the hint suggests that he is also penetrating hidden thoughts and hidden intentions. Comparing Socrates to a flutist producing the delirium of the Corybantes in his listeners—without benefit of flute or syrinx, ἄνευ ὀργάνων, ψιλοῖς λόγοις (without instruments, but with words only)—Alcibiades treats the great ironist like a Silene, that is, like a mask behind which divine figures are hidden.[10]

Nonetheless, words in themselves already signify something: their natural associations and their traditions resist the arbitrary and limit our interpretive liberty. The language of a hermetic orator who speaks in veiled words also possesses a literal sense. But music? Directly, in itself, music signifies nothing, unless by convention or association. Music means nothing and yet means everything. One can make notes say what one will, grant them any power of analogy: they do not protest. In the very measure that one is inclined to attribute a metaphysical significance to musical discourse, music (which expresses no communicable sense) lends itself, complaisant and docile, to the most complex dialectical interpretations. In the very measure that one tends to confer upon music the dimension of depth, music is, perhaps, the most superficial form of appearance.

Music has broad shoulders. In the hermeneutics of music, everything is possible, the most fabulous ideologies and unfathomable imputed meanings. Who will ever give us the lie?

Music "created the world" says Alexander Blok, the famous Russian poet: it is the essence of the spiritual body, of the flow of thought. True, Blok is himself a *poet*, and we know that poets are licensed to say everything. Schopenhauer's "metaphysics of music" has often been criticized, sometimes at the cost of overlooking its complex and original intuitions.

It is critical to point out, however, that all such *metamusic*, music thus romanticized, is at once arbitrary and metaphorical. It is arbitrary because one cannot see exactly what justifies taking the acoustic universe and privileging and promoting it to this degree above all others. Why should hearing, alone among all the senses, have the privilege of accessing the "thing in itself" for us, and thus destroy the limits of our finitude? What monopoly will enable certain perceptions, those we call auditory, those alone, to be uncapped into the realm of noumena? Will it be necessary (as was once the case) to draw a fine distinction between primary and secondary characteristics? And why (if you will) should our critical faculties, which pull our thinking back within the phenomenal world, be somehow suspended for the sake of pure sound sensations, sensations that are above all subject to the temporal? We would understand this favoritism toward sounds if time were the essence of being and the most real reality: this is what Bergson says, but not what Schopenhauer says, not at all. Besides, if this were the case, human beings—beings in the state of Becoming—would not need music to penetrate "in medias res." The temporal being would swim among noumena like a fish in water. On the other hand, is it enough that musical perception be scheduled and regulated by high art for that order to acquire an ontological impact? In that case, however, one cannot understand why the metaphysics of poetry has not enjoyed the same privilege as the metaphysics of music, nor why the conceits of poet-metaphysicians would not be as justified as the reveries of metaphysicians writing on music and musicians. In short, what must be argued over is music's "realism"—in this instance, the privilege enjoyed by a kind of more-than-phenomenal music that is the immediate objectification of the Will, and whose developments recapitulate the sad avatars of the Will.

On the other hand, the metaphysics of music is not constructed without recourse to many analogies and metaphorical transpositions: the correspondences between musical discourse and our subjective lives, between the assumed structures of Being and musical discourse, and between the structures of Being and our subjective lives as mediated by musical discourse. A first example of such analogies: the polarity of major and minor corresponds to that of the two great "ethoi" of subjective mood, serenity and depression. Dissonance tends toward consonance through cadences and appogiaturas, and consonance troubled anew by dissonance allegorizes human disquiet and a human desire that oscillates ceaselessly between wish and surfeit. By such means, the philosophy of music reduces itself in part to a metaphorical psychology of desire. Another analogy: the superimposition of singing above bass sonorities, of melody and harmony, corresponds to the cosmological gamut of beings, with consciousness at the peak and inorganic material at the base. By such means music becomes evolutionary psychology.

But, for all that, Schopenhauer himself does not fall into psychologism since (for him) music has become metaphysics just as metaphysics has become in some way musical. Ultimately, the psychological drama of the individual recapitulates the odyssey of a specific Will, unless the metaphysical odyssey itself constitutes the extension of a psychological drama, of a series of privileged states of the soul. When music is involved, the graphical and spatial transcription of sound successions greatly facilitates this extension of the psychological drama.[11] Melodic lines ascend and descend—on staff paper, but not in the world of sound, which has neither "up" nor "down." The staff is a spatial projection of the distinction between high and

sound, between bass and soprano; the simultaneous
:es in polyphony appear "superior" or "inferior" according
.. .he geologist's model of superimposed strata, and hence
also the "stratification" of consciousness. The realm of super-
sensible music itself, by means of a double illusion, ends by
appearing to be situated "beyond" the most stratospheric high
regions of audible music; the ultraphysics of the metamusical
thus takes on a naively topographical sense. Bergson de-
finitively refuted visual myths and metaphors that confer the
three dimensions of the optical and kinesthetic universe on
the temporal. The translation of duration in terms of volume
makes speculations relating to musical transcendence so illusory. Space and time are not themselves more symmetrical
than past and future are within time itself; the singular character of musical temporality makes a castle in Spain of all the
architectonic philosophy that is built upon such temporality.
The "metaphysics of music," like magic or arithmatology, always loses sight of the function of metaphors and the symbolic relativity of symbols. A sonata *is like* a précis of the
human adventure that is bordered by death and birth—but is
not *itself* this adventure. The *Allegro maestoso* and the Adagio—Schopenhauer wants to write their metaphysics—are
like a stylization of the two tempos of experienced time, but
they are not themselves this time itself. The sonata, the symphony, and the string quartet, moreover, are like a thirty-min-
ute recapitulation of the metaphysical and noumenal destiny
of the Will but are by no means this destiny per se. Everything
hangs upon the meaning of the verb *to be* and the adverb *like*,
and just as sophisms and puns slip without warning from
unilateral attribution to ontological identity—that is, make
discontinuity disappear magically—so metaphysical-meta-
phorical analogies about music slip furtively from figural
meaning to correct and literal meaning. Thus, anthropomor-
phic and anthroposophic generalizations are shameless in ignoring the restrictive clause on images and take comparisons

at face value. Being-in-itself ascends the five lines of the staff. It is the ontological evil of existing—and no longer just Chaikovsky's pessimism—that is expressed in the key of E minor. More generally, the musical microcosm reproduces, in miniature, the hierarchies of the cosmos. It will not seem sufficient to say that musical discourse "plays out" the vicissitudes of Will, if one's ambition is to attribute some magical value to such associations.

Everyday things sometimes impose visual metaphors upon us, and Bergson himself had no qualms about differentiating between the "superficial" self and the "deep" self. But *only* an awareness that a way of speaking is, simply, a way of speaking can keep us honest. A metaphysics of music that claims to transmit messages from the other world retraces the incantatory action of enchantment upon the enchanted in the form of an illicit relocation of the here-and-now to the Beyond. Sophism gets extended by means of a swindle. As a result, this metaphysics is clandestine twice over. I would conclude, therefore, that music is not above all laws and not exempt from the limitations and servitude inherent in the human condition. And, finally, that if "ethics" of music is a verbal mirage, "metaphysics" of music is closer to being a mere rhetorical figure.

THE INEXPRESSIVE "ESPRESSIVO"

THE MIRAGE OF DEVELOPMENT. THE REPRISE

No one has ever harbored loftier notions of autonomous musical reality than Schopenhauer, so we may well be surprised that, while affirming the independence of music from drama, he nonetheless charges music with the expression of a supramusical reality—metaphysical as this reality may be—and puts music in service of the quintessence of essences. In effect, this metaphysical prejudice relies on the notion that music is a language, a sort of encrypted language, whose alphabet is the notes of the scale. Language is the mode of human expression par excellence, the one most easy to handle and most voluble, but it is not the only such mode. Human beings are talking animals and only secondarily animals that sing. Music says what logos says (whether the words are occult or transparent), but music says it in the form of sound hieroglyphs. Music says in singing what the word says in saying.

As it happens, it is the entire Western notion of "development" in music, of fugue and sonata form, that has thus been influenced by the assumptions of rhetoric. Just as there is a "train" of thought, a reasoning process that progresses and

unfolds all implications of meaning, there must be (to speak
with Ansermet), a musical path, an itinerary, along which
musical themes develop. Is a symphony a form of discourse?
Is a sonata comparable to a closing argument? Fugue a disser-
tation, oratorio a sermon? Do the themes in a symphony play
the same role as the "ideas" in an academic's lecture? Clearly,
these references to "development" are manners of speaking,
metaphors and analogies, dictated to us by our habitual discursive ways. In comparison to forms of intentional signification, music operates according to a completely different plan:
thus by means of a manner of speaking, to stabilize his or her
ideas, a listener hearing symphony pretends to "follow" the
development of a musical idea. What do I mean by this? As
regards the unfolding of any single general idea, any abstract
concept, *preamble* and *conclusion* are themselves metaphorical
notions. Where a spatializing and associative intelligence,
skimming over this unfolding, distinguishes several sections
framed by an exordium and a peroration, the ear—caught in
the immediacy and innocence of succession as experienced
live—does not perceive such things at all. Without a retrospective envisaging of the path that was followed, pure audition would not notice the form of the sonata. For this "plan"
is a something conceived, and not at all something heard, not
time subjectively experienced. The melancholy, the smooth
dreaminess that Slavic musicians (Anton Dvořák, Chaikovsky)
call *dumka* is not a thought (*duma*) but a "little thought," a
nascent and groping thought, the opposite of a rigorous sequence. Even when it resembles the narrative ballad of Ukrai-
nian folklore, the dumka keeps its twilit, diffuse character.
The meditative musical reverie is not "meditative" except in a
manner of speaking, because it has no object on which it
meditates and never untangles the consequences implicit in an
idea.

    In the "stationary" music of the twentieth century, *Pe-
trushka*, *Les Noces*, *El retablo de Maese Pedro*, a phobia of de-

velopment results from a kind of fierce continence. The *Cirandas* of Villa-Lobos in this respect are truly obsessive. This is stationary music, stagnant music, but not at all static. The refusal to develop, the will to strangle eloquence, occasionally extends to heroic extremes: the taste for short, disjointed phrases in Musorgsky, Debussy's brachylogy: do they not represent—in opposition to all rhetoric, all oratorical ambitions—the regime of the "interrupted serenade"?[1] In Debussy, the interruption of the serenade will be more an effect of modesty, understated humor. In Musorgsky, it results from a need for discontinuity: *Il vecchio castello*, interrupted serenade, breaks off and dwindles away into the night without having developed or amplified its romance; the sobs of the mandolin withdraw little by little, and finally silence submerges them. Louis Vuillemin's atmospheric poems in this way rise in spirals into space. Thus, in Ravel, lingers the lament of those *Oiseaux tristes*. But Debussy's Piano Preludes, and even *La Mer*, despite all their agitation, are they not oddly stagnant? The intrinsic inaptitude for development can explain at least two essential traits of all musical "discourse": its absence of any systematic unity, and its insensitivity to repetition.

The musical universe, not signifying any particular meaning, is first of all the antipode to any coherent system. The philosopher who reflects upon the world aspires at the very least to coherence in attempting to resolve contradictions, reduce the irreducible, to integrate the necessary evils of duality and plurality. Music ignores such concerns since it does not have ideas to line up logically with one another. Harmony itself is less the rational synthesis of opposites than the irrational symbiosis of the heterogeneous. Is it not harmony that, in Plato, causes contradictory virtues to reconcile and agree among themselves? The experienced simultaneity of opposites is the daily regime, incomprehensible as it might be, of a life full of music. Music, like movement or duration, is a continuous miracle that with every step accomplishes the impossible. The superimposed voices of polyphony realize a *concordia discors*, of which music alone is capable, because intelligent articulation based on reciprocity, because the meshed gears of question and answer in a dialogue, differ as much from the synchronism of heterogeneous voices in counterpoint as the "harmony" one produces by adjudication differs from musical harmony. Words carry meaning, and two interlocutors cannot speak simultaneously without the threat of confusion because several simultaneous monologues produce nothing more than nameless cacaphony; people who speak with one another must do so successively, and it is this alternation that constitutes dialogue. But "ensemble" in a chorus assumes the mutual fit of all parties with one another according to a different rule: is this not the organic *consensus* whose name is Concert?

True, certain piano works by Federico Mompou, and by Chaikovsky (op. 72, no. 8), bear the name *Dialogue*:[2] but these are fictive discussions and conversations as metaphorical as those in Ravel's duo between Beauty and the Beast.[3] In Bartók's four "Dialogues," the two hands are not saying anything to one another. Nor are the two violins in the *Quarante-quatre Duos*. Nor are the violin and the cello in Ravel's duo sonata.[4]

Even the extraordinarily moving "dialogue" of the piano and the orchestra in César Franck's *Variations symphoniques* is more alternation of melodies than exchange of "thoughts." In piano four-hands or two-piano music, in Bizet's *Petit mari, petite femme*, or in the piece by Fauré entitled *Tendresse*, that which imitates dialogues does so only metaphorically.[5] No less metaphorical is "Question and Response" from Hugo Wolf's *Mörike-Lieder*: here we have a question that risks remaining eternally unanswered.[6] Because there never was (in all likelihood) a question at all, this particular "question" risks being eternally suspended, just like Schumann's "Warum?" in the *Fantasiestücke*: forever interrogative. It has been said that the symmetry of question and response in the sixteenth quartet of Beethoven ("Muss es sein? Es muss sein!") lays bare a music that is like discursive language, capable of opposing a thesis and an antithesis, "of developing them and concluding not with a synthesis but with well-conceived affirmation."[7] It is hard to imagine someone being more profoundly deceived by the rhetoric of transposition. Even the correlation between two motifs, one ascending, one descending, in Rimsky's *Coq d'or*, even this has a character that is more graphic and visual than auditory. Is symmetry not the spatial projection of the temporal process of becoming? Music is familiar with the echo, which is the melody's mirror-reflection of itself, and with canonic imitation, but it knows nothing of dialogue. In polyphony, the voices speak together, harmoniously, but they are not speaking among themselves *to one another*, they are not addressing themselves *to one another*: they are singing in concert for an outsider, like choristers who turn toward a listener. Or who attest to the presence of God. In a duet, the impulse does not really pass, transitively, from one voice to the other but more from the two singers to the listener. Could one say, therefore, that there is a transitive and intentional relationship between performer and listener? In fact, a singer in a duet does not address him or herself any more to the public than to his or her partner: if the correlation between the correlatives is not direct, there is also no unmediated relationship between the performers and the listeners. The singer may well look at me while her mouth is open in song, but she does not *speak*, not to me. The horn sonorities at the beginning of Fauré's *Pelléas* are not calling me personally, and the raucous cry in the second of Ravel's *Chansons madécasses* is not apostrophizing any particular individual among all those who hear it: no one is designated by the cry; it concerns no one. Allocution—the communication of meaning and the transmission of intentions—is out of a job where music is concerned. Someone who talks to nobody is mad. Someone who sings to nobody, as if he were a bird, without addressing anyone, is just happy. One doesn't "listen to" a pianist playing *before* his public or a

singer singing before this same public in the same way that
one "listens to" a lecturer speaking to his audience, because
for the lecturer the listener is the second person—"you," the
object of invocation or allocution—whereas the listener is the
third person, the outsider, for the pianist sitting at the piano.
Transfixed by the spotlight and isolated on the platform, the
pianist and the singer are, in relation to the listener, a spectacle in and of themselves. The listener-observer remains isolated from this soliloquy without interlocutors, this sonata.
He is no longer an interlocutor, but an outsider, a witness.
A musical work is of course not bound by any ideological coherence. It is this feature that no doubt explains—from the
standpoint of the listener—the pluralism of aesthetic tastes, as
opposed to the sporadic nature of evident truths, in music.
This disjunction has nothing in to do either with dilettantism
in general or with confused eclecticism. One cannot profess
several contradictory dogmas simultaneously, but one may
take pleasure in dissimilar qualities, in differing and irrecon-
cilable genres of beauty. One can love Franck and Debussy
without having to justify that love, which is never a form of
incoherence.

That which cannot "say" anything cannot a fortiori repeat.
Thus, is repetition in music not a priori a shock, are the re-
frains and ritornellos of strophic song, or the periodic recur-
rences of rondo form, not also a shock? Fauré certainly renounced the strophic symmetry of the *Lied*, and Debussy
renounced the lockstep of harmony; and in general contemporary music, hungry for rejuvenation and perpetual originality, bans all manner of harping, thus willing itself to become an image of life, spontaneous outpouring and progress
that cannot be foreseen.

But the repeat in music—is it sterile? First of all, there is
the echo, whose importance in the music of a Séverac or a
Georges Migot is patent, and which is the direct opposite of a
pleonasm, of a simple refolding, something facile. Whether

the second occurrence involves a pianissimo (or not), if it has taken place an octave below (or above) or on the same scale degree, the second occurrence provides a continuation to the semelfactive instant and allows it to survive; it surrounds a solitary voice with amity, fraternal company, and sympathy. Just as, in Pushkin, poets echo Nature and Nature echoes human singing, so music echoes itself (see Rimsky's op. 45, no. 1). The second time around, the inchoate musical phrase becomes organic; the second time around, that which was arbitrary and unusual assumes a more profound sense.

And it can happen, as in Satie's obsessive music, or Stravinsky's or Villa-Lobos's, or in Janáček's operas, that reiteration itself exerts an increasing power of bewitchment. "Gnossian" time, in Satie, turns a mesmerized consciousness into stone. The sorcery of De Falla's *El amor brujo*, or the incatatory power of the *Fantasia baetica*, is inherent in the very lack of progress. Between first and second occurrences, an interval of time has passed that renews the iterated sound and makes an incantation out of insistence, magic out of monotony, progress out of stationary repetition. Did Bergson not demonstrate how each tick of a clock, succeeding those that preceded it in time, qualitatively changes the listener's past? If the repeat is immediate and literal, if the "reprise" pure and simple can, in music, be a form of rejuvenation, it will play a fortiori the same part in the case of the recapitulation or the resurgence of themes in cyclic works. It is in prose discourse that repetitions are proscribed: because discourse, whether it develops a meaning, whether it lays out or demonstrates a thesis, proceeds from the beginning by means of dialectical progress, and steers, quite rightly, without returning or going back. Here, what has been said is no longer to be said; what is said is definitive: one time is sufficient. To start again would be odious, just as a joke too often repeated by a professional comedian becomes useless and distressing. The already-said is itself grounds for not re-saying. Thus logos condemns the re-

peat, just as it condemns all senile stammering, all that is The
involuntary assonance or idée fixe: they are reversions to par-
rotry and automatism, to materiality. Didactic language has
an object: the communication of truth. It does not seek incantatory effects, by means of litanies or accumulations.

Nonetheless, one needs to distinguish here between the creator's point of view and that of the reader: for the creator, a
repeat is a reassessment. For the reader, it may be a pedagogic
necessity demanded by our slowness in comprehending, our
lack of concentration or mental deafness. In addition, it can
happen that deep meaning forces us to circle in place; the
reader thus sinks deeper and deeper instead of moving on.

In music and in poetry, to the contrary, reiteration may
constitute an innovation for the creator as well as for the listener or the reader. One would criticize a mathematician or a
civil code for saying the same thing twice when saying it once
is sufficient. But one does not reproach a Psalmist for repeat-
ing himself—because he aims to create religious obsession in
us and not to develop ideas; his art of persuasion is passionate
and not apodictic. One cannot criticize Janáček's *Glagolithic
Mass* for its "monotony" because it employs a kind of enveloping rhetoric whose effects extend to the sublime. In the
"development" based on signification, what is said is not to be
re-said; in music and poetry, what is said remains to be said,
and to be said without cessation, inexhaustibly said. To remain silent, in this domain, under the pretext that "everything has been said" is a sophism in substance and quan-
titatively, as much as refusing to write a poem about love
because the subject has already been dealt with. *Premier amour*:
this is the title Turgenev gives to a story whose atmosphere
invokes springtime and inconsolable nostalgia. Love comes into
being, irreversibly: this "semelfactive" love, is it not always
first and brand new, for the one experiencing it? Inexhaustible
(like love), tireless (like nature), and eternally young (like
spring): this is the Charm that operates in poetic rhythms, as

The
Inexpressive
"Espressivo"

23

it appears to us, operating incessantly, reborn again in its eternal newness, in infinity, for a reader who is never satiated.

To recreate in this case is to create, just as to re-make is to make, to begin again to begin—the second time being as initial as the first, the recapitulation as initial as the exposition. In a sonata, where there are no "ideas" to develop (except metaphorically), the recapitulation is not a "repeat" but instead a principle of order: the form is made manifest to us by the regularity of the gesture, which gives the illusion of symmetry, of a closed system or a "circuit."[8] To *re-expose* a theme means lending it a new sense and new illumination exclusively because of the subsequent moment where the reappearance manifests itself. In the irreversibility of Becoming,[9] every event—as much as it may be identical to its predecessors— takes over from them. The *second time* in a Rondo, even if it does not differ from the first time except by the ordinal number, nevertheless engenders the anterior quality of the first in the midst of a context that always changes. Independent of any concrete memory, the pure fact of succession and the preterite, in other words the naked past-ness of the past, prevents the "same" from remaining exactly the same; this continuous conditioning, in the process of Becoming, assumes the form of a continuous alteration. This is why the da capo is a ravishing surprise, why a theme does not give up all that stirs us in its meaning until it is recognized once again. Do recapitulations not activate a form of memory within us? In concrete terms, the return of the theme signifies, to quote Gisèle Brelet, the poetry of recollection, fulfilled expectation, the joy of finding a friend whom one had missed. For the listener and the performer, the reprise is no less a renewal: hearing again, playing again, become modes whereby to discover, interminably, new relationships or subtle correspondences, beauty kept secret or hidden intentions. The polyphonic superimposition of several independent voices that are nonetheless arranged in accord with one another, the multivocal ambiguity that results, the innuendos and allusions that accumulate in these superimposed levels, the unsaid things that they conceal like hidden treasure—in these no doubt there is a source of inexhaustible pleasure. *Decies repetita placebit*, says Henri Bremond.[9] If all these riches are experienced each time cumulatively, with simple feeling, then that emotion itself, in the course of time, will continuously change color.

THE ILLUSION OF EXPRESSION

Incapable of developing in the true sense, music is—despite appearances—also incapable of expressing. In this regard we are once more the dupes of our own expressionist prejudices: we declare that music shall be, like all other languages, the bearer of meaning and an instrument of communication, whether it explains certain ideas, or suggests certain sentiments, or describes landscapes or things, or narrates events. Say it with flowers, say it with songs. Or say it in Esperanto, because there is a musical "language" in the same sense that there is a language of flowers or a hundred other enciphered languages or sign systems, and there will also be things that one cannot say except in singing or by declaiming them as poetry. Just as the organist, to express himself, makes use of his organ or the violinist her violin, so meaning, to make itself manifest, makes use of various alphabets and dialects, among others, the language of music; the means of expression we call "music" shall be at the service of the instrumentalist named "thought" in the same way that musical instruments themselves are at the disposal of the musicians. The signifying intention, then, in the very end, is the instrumentalist who trumps all other instrumentalists.

This instrumental and "utilitarian" expressionism presupposes the precedence and the hegemony of guiding intellect, that is, the logical and reasoning aspect of our soul. One must conceive before speaking, just as one must deliberate before one decides, and the signs are always subordinates. Moreover if music is thus simple language, meaning will preexist in a direct line to this language, which will constitute the second-level explanation of that meaning. Thus, anterior to the music that sounds in reality, the acoustic phenomenon that is perceptible to the human ear, there would have to exist a supra-sensible, supra-audible music, something like lost, wandering music, music anterior not only to instruments capable of playing it but to the creator capable of composing it, music anterior to the first sounding pipe as to the first vibrating string, music free, in short, to sing or not sing. Before the physical phenomenon, there would be a metaphysical music—whether metamusic or ultramusic, perfectly silent music that is indifferent to any particular expression. And finally, the music heard in reality would be—in relation to this music—more a disturbance or an impoverishment than a real means of expression. *Omnis determinatio est negatio*: the flute that channels the "artificial sigh, divine and serene," in short, limits this infinite music; and similarly the auditory conductor, in receiving the sound wave emitted by the instrument, shrinks the inaudible music to make it available to our perception.

Under these circumstances, one is led to ask whether our ears, far from being organs of hearing, are not rather more the cause of our deafness: does physiological hearing place us in communication with the world of sound or bar us from the music of the angels? Allow us to hear perceptible music or prevent us from grasping intelligible music? The organ becomes a screen, the good conductor becomes an interceptor, the positive turns to a negative—these paradoxes bear witness to a truly expressionist perversion of relations between physical senses and the sign.

The transcendence that is ascribed to intention, does it not recall—more than is quite comfortable—the ideological motivations, the utilitarian or rational conventions of the Common Sense School?[10] Man makes use of song and does not want song to make use of him. The musical idea is independent of this instrument or that, that is to say, of this or that determined mode of expression, of the human voice, piano, organ, or orchestra—but it is not independent of all sounding expression in general. Music can pass by means of transcription from one instrument to another without necessarily changing its character. We know how Ravel, how Liszt himself, virtuoso of the paraphrase and the "rearrangement," freely embraced successive versions of the same work. If the majority of musicians compose like Stravinsky, at the piano, "in direct contact with the sounding material," others compose without an instrument, and thus in some sense in the abstract.[11]

Nonetheless, the idea of an absolutely tacit music, unexpressed, disembodied, is in the very end a conceptual abstraction. The confused rumor made by the Invisible City of Kitezh would not begin to exist musically were it not for some oboes and violins that graciously consent to remain small minded. Above all, to imagine a composer straining to express something as analogous to an organist who has everything—stops, pedals, and keyboards—at his sovereign disposal, is to fail to recognize the effect of the tool on the worker, what one could call a reverse shock.

The musical act, like the creation of poetry, renders plausible at any time the paradox inherent in an ambiguous and bilateral etiology: Bergson, speaking of free acts, has cast a certain light on the amphibolic character of causality.[12] To a certain extent, the physiological theory of emotions has accustomed us to this same reversal. No cause is ever absolutely a cause, in the unilateral and unequivocal sense that Aristotle's prime mover is purely moving. Or in the sense that the Act is pure agency, or in the sense that the *causa sui* of the mystics, by virtue of its very aseity, is but the effect of itself. Because down here on earth there is no gratuitous action; no cause is entirely the cause, and no effect is exclusively an effect: rather, every cause is simultaneously to a certain extent the effect of its own effect, just as every driving force, in this relative world, is up to a certain point a driven force, and every agent up to a certain point is acted upon. The poetic act does not stand in relation to a single unique meaning, in a one-sided and irreversible subordination, but to a mutuality of multiple correlations. In this act, downward-moving causality and its inversion, upward-moving effect, expression and counter-expression, the direct and efferent wave and the induced wave, superimpose themselves upon one another and interfere with one another.

So, too, the sounding material does not simply tag along after the human mind and is not just something at the disposition of our whims. It is recalcitrant. Sometimes it refuses to take us where we would like to go; better still, this instrument, which is often an obstacle, takes us somewhere else, ushers us into the presence of beauty not foreseen. And just as the ivory of the keys possesses in and of itself qualities that inspire the person improvising at the piano, thus musical language in general suggests in turn a meaning that it was not specifically our intention to communicate. Far from being amenable to the winds of our desire, this servant of intention will make use of its own master. The material is neither a docile instrument nor a pure obstacle.

Musical improvisation as a phenomenon demonstrates this circular causality, where sign and meaning are in turn effect and cause, and demonstrates it experimentally—by the action itself—just as Achilles demonstrates the possibility of movement by moving and catches up with the famous tortoise in defiance of sophism, thus banishing the paralyzing aporias of Zeno's paradox.[13] Aristotle, denying at once the priority of an apprenticeship in praxis, and the priority of praxis in apprenticeship, concluded that doing and learning are contemporaneous:[14] because if μαθόντας ποιεῖν (to do, having learned) is an intellectual prejudice, ποιήσαντας μανθάνειν (to learn,

Chapter

Two

28

having done) is an absurdity; what is real is the synchronism
of ποιοῦντας μανθάνειν (to learn while doing) and μανθά-
νοντας ποιεῖν (to do while learning). One becomes a kithara
player in playing the kithara, just as one deliberates by choos-
ing or one thinks by saying. And it is by wanting that one
learns to want. Alain also said, "One learns by trying, and not
by thinking that one is trying."

And similarly the poet will never conceive his poem in advance of making it but in the act of making it, because in
poetry there is no gap between speculation and action, no
distance, no temporal interval. To create, one must create: it is
this vicious circle, worthy of Monsieur de la Palisse, that signifies not just that creation always begins with itself but also,
and as a consequence, that there is no recipe for learning to
create. The creator sets down essence conjointly with existence, possibility at the same time as reality.

IMPRESSIONISM

Meaning in music, for the composer, crops up as the music is
being written; for the performer and the listener, it is mani-
fested during the performance. Sporadically, then, meaning
will emanate from a work evolving through and in time. Even
more than instrumental music, singing bears witness to the
narrow interaction between meaning and act. This is because
the human voice is only a "natural instrument" in a manner
of speaking, just as a human organ is a natural tool or a tool
an artificial organ, only metaphorically. Singing is the immediate and unpremeditated extension of intention, of which it
is at once expressive and constitutive. A human being that
sings expresses him- or herself through pure efferent spontaneity, apart from any utility or rational argument.

If music does not express ideas, shall it become instead the
language of sentiments and passions? More than prose, more
even than poetry, shall it be a means to transmit secrets or

avowals concerning the affective intimate core of its creator? This was the Romantic view, or at least, it was the view purveyed by the Romantics when, ex post facto, they interpreted their works for their public. The explicit intention to confide: is it present in the moment? I have my doubts. Paul Dukas speaks of the degeneration that began in the nineteenth century, and that made music into psychological tragedies, transposed. And more generally, the musicians of the twentieth century, glad to be unjust vis-à-vis the romantic *Espressivo*, make fun of the preference for unambiguous "expression" at every possible turn. "Expression," says Stravinsky, "has never been an immanent property of music."[15] This is Roland-Manuel's opinion as well.

Be that as it may, anti-Romanticism's reaction against the expressionist fury has taken two forms: the first can be called Impressionism, the second, a search for the inexpressive. At the outset, picturesque Impressionism could function as a diversion from the expressionist humoresque; the impression, which is sensory but objective, decharges the expression, which is exhibitionistic and subjective. The impression, which is centripetal, lowers the temperature on the soul and its pathos, and attenuates the need for effusion through the will to detachment. Our introverted consciousness liberates itself, thanks to atmospheric impressions. Intense music, music befitting an unhappy soul, would come to know a state of détente, thanks to open air and open sky. Bartók gives the title *Out of Doors* to a collection of six pieces in which the sounds of the night answer the fifes and drums and musettes of a country village. Monsieur Croche, antidilettante, vows to reclaim music that would play and hover in the branches of the trees and in the light of the free air; this vow is redeemed by Bartók as well as the Impressionists. In other words, one way for human beings not to tell stories about themselves is to talk to us about "Collines d'Anacapri," or the wind on the plains or bells heard through leaves.

Being more a narrator than an impressionist, Rimsky-Korsakov was much too busy telling of the adventures of Sadko, the miracles of Tzar Saltan, or Sheherazade's astonishing marvels, to make confidences about his coronary irregularities; confession is not his forte. Acute sensibility to a certain extent neutralizes ardent sentimentality. These "impressions" are short-lived, as short-lived as the twenty fugitive moods that Prokofiev assembles in his *Mimolyotnosti* (*Visions fugitives*). "In each and every fleeting instant," writes Russian poet Konstantin Balmont, "I see worlds full of shifting and iridescent interplay." The explicit intention to alternate such "humors" or "moods" already implies an imperceptible measure of humor: because if there is one mood, there are many, there are innumerable moods, and they give lie to one another. A smile effaces itself, like a sun that clouds over, and tears succeed it; the tears and the smiles are merely episodes in one's emotional life. Consciousness surveys the procession of contradictory impressions in this voyage through the moods, skims them from above, and will thus realize the precise limits of each quotidian "impression," and at the same time transcend the impassioned eternity of sentiment.

Sentiment (being a chronic state), does it not suggest the perennial, that which lingers, the slow impregnation of all consciousness? True, the Appassionato, the sonatas and symphonies that are "pathétiques," also imply the instability characteristic of the humoresque: but the moods in the sentimental humoresque are convinced that they are eternal and absolute, while those in the humorous humoresque know that they are provisional. Debussy's *Preludes* do not allow the life of the affects any time for lingering. Similarly, in the miniscule and miniature tableaux of Federico Mompou, in Janáček's *Řikadla*, as in Stravinsky's *Pribautki* or his "Berceuses de Chat," in Satie's *Sports et divertissements*, brachylogy signifies a fear of pressing, the concern never to insist. With Debussy, the "Moment musicale"[16] becomes a musical *instant*. Because "imn" is, already, reticence in the face of the Appas-

THE INEXPRESSIVE AND OBJECTIVITY

Just as Debussy's impressionism reacts against the debaucheries of expressionism, so the inexpressive style, in Ravel and Satie, sometimes reacts against the delights of impressionism. Just as impressionism's scintilla, its gold power, riddled the cumulus of Romantic piano pedaling with luminous stings, so the object itself now parcels out its keen edges as vagueness and blur, as Debussyian "Mists."[1] Inexpressive realism inscribes itself as the scything-down of expressionist truthfulness.[18] The expressionist expressed sentiments having to do with sensation; the impressionist takes note of his sensations about things; and inexpressive music allows things themselves to speak, in their primal rawness, without necessitating intermediaries of any kind. The ambition of hyperrealism is in effect to reduce to a minimum the role of stylization or transposition inherent in all artistic intention. Philosophy, returning to the "concrete" (according to Jean Wahl's expression), takes an analogous step towards things *themselves*: as much as academic idealism sees things from a distance, so Bergson's pure perception or N. O. Lossky's intuition establish themselves not just in the immediate proximity of things but face to face with the real *just as* it is, *at the real*: it is no longer an immediate and objective given that stands in front of you, but nature *in person*.

"As if you were there yourself": this is what Musorgsky, writing to Vladimir Stasov, calls truth at point-blank range.[19] Naked truth stripped of all rhetoric, truth in flesh and bone, raw, incoherent truth, the truth of the gossips that caw in the market at Limoges, of Cossacks, Jews, and Gypsies who squabble at the Sorochintsï Fair, the naive truth of the child who converses with his ragdoll, all these real noises, raw and na-

ked, are immediately present in Musorgsky's music: their un-
couth ingenuity did not have to run through thickets of symbols, nor through the idealizing and stylizing distance that art
interposes between the mind and the noises of the world.

Musorgsky's music gets right to the point: disdaining pref-
aces, preliminaries, and middle terms that would prolong the
route, how could such innocent music—music without a detour—be anything but extraordinarily concise? *Boris Godunov*
reduces the prelude to a minimum and throws us right into
the middle of the action. *Chose en soi:* maybe Prokofiev, in
giving this bizarre title to two piano pieces in his op. 45, just
wanted to pique our curiosity.[20] Because these "things-in-
themselves," at an opposite pole to the picturesque, are particularly abstract sonorous combinations, formal and arid. Yet
perhaps in op. 45 Prokofiev was seeking a pure musical object
without passing through the deforming a priori of affective
psychology. The composer-genius who wrote *Pas d'acier* knew
the most direct route to find and touch the immediate. In this
"steel dance," one hears the brutal percussion of hammers
just as on hears the cannon shots in Shostakovich's Symphony
XI or the horns of the cars in Gershwin. As one hears the roar
of motors in Mosolov's *The Foundry*. The atonal racket of the
machines resounds *as it is* in these precursors of true "musique concrète."

And analogously, it is bells themselves that ring in Louis
Vuillemin's *Soirs armoricains*—and not, as with the Romantics, an idealist, subjective transposition of the poetry of bell
sounds: the bronze fourths resonate directly in the piano,
with their dissonant overtones. Stravinsky's nightingale is a
real nightingale that sings a real nightingale song, a nonmusical song, and not some more or less humanized and stylized
vocalization. Albert Roussel, in *Rossignol mon mignon*, fur-
nishes us with another example: there is a "real" nightingale
who, through the medium of the flute's agile voice, entwines
its trills and fioratura with human singing. The ballet of little

birds in Musorgsky's *Pictures at an Exhibition,* in its acidity and stridence, with realism has become a little sour, is in contrast to the melodiousness and musicality of the birds that one hears in Liszt's *St. François d'Assise,* in the same way that Stravinsky's nightingale contrasts to the harmonious nightingales of Rimsky-Korsakov. Messiaen's *Catalogue des oiseaux,* without the literary onomatopoeias or imitative conventions of a Daquin or a Saint-Saens, wants to be a faithful notation of real birdsong. With the Romantics or with Novak,[21] the two melancholy notes of the cuckoo in a deep wood expressed— via the movement of a descending third—the nostalgia of a human being who feels moved when, at evening, he senses the scent of spring. But today's composers shut out any form of too-human languor. It is the crickets themselves who drone in Bartók's "The Night's Music" (*Out of Doors,* no. 4). Above all, the animal populace perform their animal symphony, a cacophony, but hardly a coarse one: Janáček's *The Cunning Little Vixen,* Ravel's *Histoires naturelles* and *L'Enfant et les Sortilèges. Les Oiseaux et les bêtes:* a wonderful melody from northern Russia, harmonized by Balakirev, could also serve as the epigraph to Ravel's *Histoires naturelles,* to the *Forêt bleue* of Louis Aubert, and to the *Petit Poucet* where one hears the peeping of goldcrests and tits. The peacock who shrieks, the cat who meows, the frogs who croak, the chittering of nocturnal insects, the swishing sounds of fireflies, the cackling of pigeons and the chirp of June bugs make themselves heard, here, in their brute truthfulness.

Maurice Ravel gave speech not only to animals but to plants and to inanimate things, to discordant clocks, a fire that hisses and crackles: the tree itself, and not some secondary phantom of a tree, groans and complains, when Ravel makes the portando of the flora manifest to the ear, in that moonlit garden. And nonetheless, as Roland-Manuel pointed out, Ravel is not among those who draw from the "dictionary of nature."

The most striking consequence of this objectivism is the

erasure of the human figure. The seascapes, the impressionist

"exteriors" in Gabriel Dupont's *La Maison dans les dunes*, are
all inhabited by memory, by the "melancholy of happiness,"
and the landscapes in *Les Heures dolentes*, which constitute
the diary of a sickness, are all states of the soul. Behind the
Chanson du vent and the *Chanson de la pluie* (*Les Heures dolentes*, nos. 4 and 8), can one not sense both the motif, and the
anguish, of death? In "Mon frère le vent et ma soeur la pluie"
(*La Maison dans les dunes*, no. 4), the malady of solitude bears
witness to its kinship with the elements. The solitary human
being is always present when "sun plays on the waves" when
the "rumor of the sea and night" is heard, when the inhuman
swell of the ocean rumbles. With Déodat de Séverac, the presence of a woman, the "charming encounter" with the beloved,
the beach-goers in the sun, almost always humanizes the décor
of Cerdagne and the Languedoc. As for the *Chant de la terre*,
it tells of labors and efforts of a people of the land.

Even with Ravel, the Child is present in the murmuring
garden as the sole representative, in his person, of the human
instance: the last word in *L'Enfant et les Sortilèges*, is it not the
impulse of the heart, which suddenly appeases the unleashed
animals? Even Bela Bartók's acid "The Night's Music" (see also
Mikrokosmos II, 63), so dissimilar to the Romantic nocturne
with its caress and its reverie, is, once more, musical noise,
harmonized noises that imply human presence: the furtive
rustlings, mysterious gruppettos, and crackling seconds and
strident upper-register octaves, bizarrely repeated notes, answer each other and propagate themselves in the vast silence
of night; in place of the lover's serenade, one hears the sigh of
the wind, the dialogue of the toad and owl; the shrill voice of
the insects echoes the rustling of the leaves. But the ento-
mological scherzo, with its perfectly nonmelodic and atonal
noisemaking, will suddenly efface itself in silence. Among all
animal, vegetable, and mineral voices, among the staccatos,
the metallic shuddering of "little animals,"[22] this is what dis-

tinguishes human singing: it has—crude as it may be—number, meter, tonality, intention. Human singing, with a solemn sadness characteristic of southern peasants, gives restful voice to melancholy, a heart that is full of night: singing that is melodious and measured is already music. Orpheus the mage is speaking, through the medium of rustic song, to the trees and the midnight insects, just as St. Francis of Assisi's voice, in Liszt's piano piece, answers the confused twittering of the swallows.

Paradoxically, however, it is with Debussy's impressionism that inexhaustible nature appears in its most immediate form, and that the truth of a blade of grass or a splash of water asserts itself to us in the most hallucinatory way of all: we live it, touch it, sense its presence in the miniscule black marks that race and shudder, like telegrams, over the staves of the *Rondes de printemps*. For Debussy is so brilliant that he outstrips even the hyperrealism of his contemporaries. To see the sunrise, he said, is more important than listening to Beethoven's *Pastoral Symphony*. Debussy put a stethoscope to the ocean's chest, to the tide's lungs, to the heart of the sea and the earth; thus his symphonic poems never behave like narrative, with proper closure. In *La Mer*, the human person's face has utterly disappeared.

La Mer, like "Le vent dans la plaine," "Ce qu'a vu le vent d'ouest," "Broulliards," or *Nuages*, is the anonymous elements' poem, the poem of inhuman meteors. The immemorial conflict depicted by *La Mer* plays itself out far from the coastal seaports and beaches and "baigneuses au soleil" and human civilization. "Jeu de vagues" is not "Jeux d'eux."[23] What *La Mer* describes for us is not the jet of water, the masterpiece of hydraulics, the svelte corolla vaporized by the art of fountain makers, but inchoate chaos and barbarous disorder, lawless agitation. Here, one hears neither the dialogue of a human being with others, nor (as in Gabriel Dupont) the dialogue of a solitary man with the solitary sea, not at all, and still less (as in Liszt) the dialogue of nature and humanity. No, there is nothing here but the dialogue of the wind and the sea, which is moreover the monologue of the ocean, excluding all anthropomorphism, all reference to the subject. The dialogue, in which interlocutors speak alternatively, each ceding to the other, and even polyphony, which brings them in concord with one another, gives way to the coexistence or copresence of all noises, universal simultaneity, a great and primitive confusion. With Vuillemin, dissonance expresses the sporadicism and incoherence of all noises. Even in Debussy's *Sirènes*, the women are not singing words: they are the collective and impersonal voice, an instrumental timbre. Sirens are the elemental sound of seduction, just as Woman, in Novák's *Pan*, is an element of the same order as Forest, Ocean, or Mountain.

The rushing of the swell in Gabriel Dupont's *La maison dans les dunes*, birdsong, or the noise of a factory, the clicking sounds of metal or the crackling sounds of wood, the lapping sound of water and the shrieks of wind, represent a kind of border zone beyond which art simply reabsorbs itself into reality. Strict objectivism, fleeing the life of the emotions and in default of expression, approaches the nonmelodic and nonmusical, the paramusical or premusical zone that is, like the ocean, the total universe of amorphous noise and chaotic rumor.

Perhaps it is in this sense that we can understand the crucial role played by the interval of the second, whether major or minor, first in Musorgsky, then in Debussy, Ravel, Szymanowski, and Bartók. The second—the inversion of the major seventh—lets the note "next to" resound; that is, it lets the wrong note sound with or very near the right one: is this second not the most undifferentiated and least harmonious of all the intervals? Closest to brute noise? The noise of things not yet understood is going to be louder than music's voice: because things, these "mute persons" (as Jean Wahl calls them) speak an unformed language that ignores the prosody and *materiality*

intonation of singing. "Diary of a Fly" with its little stings and inclement buzzing, lurks everywhere—too much so—in Bartók's music.[24] Often, the second hums in the interior of a closely spaced chord, as in those harmonies "en brouillard" that are presented in the *Mikrokosmos*. Packets of notes, gruppettos, thus create blurs and confusions.

Yet this must be said as well about the "bitonality" that allows black keys and white keys to be struck at the same time: think of Debussy's prelude from Book II, called, rightly, "Brouillards." After the white *Nuages* in the orchestral *Nocturnes*, here is the nimbus, the *Nuages gris*.[25] Paul Dukas described the end of Debussy's *Nuages* for orchestra as "gray agony lightly tinted with white."[26] "Un peu gris": we read those words at the head of Bartók's second *Burlesque* op. 8. Autumnal greyness, which has the color of dust and ashes: does it not evoke Debussyist sky? Gray represents the neutral source and informs all optical tonalities. One might say that music, for a lark, pretends to disappear into the gray ocean of prose.

At the opposite pole to all lyricism and all operatic convention, the prosaic "parlando," *sermo solutus*, in other words atonal speech, is doubtless the limit toward which absolutely objective and concrete music is inclining. Here, one does not differentiate between singing on pitch or singing off pitch; just as the major–minor distinction had effaced itself in modal music, so the univocal categories in "musical" music end in the indeterminacy of a *portando*, in which sustained intonation no longer has any meaning and in which sound in general becomes approximate. In Liszt's last works, chromaticism already led to this condition of indecisiveness; dodecaphonic music and quarter-tone music, according to the Formalists and the Abstracts, are its codification as theory.

We can consider here only one case of realism: once again, Musorgsky was the first explorer to go into the border zone. His *Marriage*, the last operas of Janáček, or Krenek's *Jonny spielt auf*, more or less stick very close—without stylized or-

naments or oratorical amplification or subjective commentary—to the graphic lines of ordinary conversation. And
somehow this music that no longer differentiates between
singing and reciting remains profoundly musical and inti-
mately emotional. Only at the moment when one reaches
things in themselves, nature's voice itself, truth itself, only
then does inexpressive music become expressive again; on the
verge of losing its actual musical character, extreme realism
becomes music again. Objective realism is an elaborate acrobatic game played with prose and the present, with that which
is insipid and without color or scent. Prose is poeticized by
the milligram of delirium that enters into any musical performance; the present is made past-like by the milligram of nostalgia, by the infinitesimal and somehow minimal regret, that
makes all perception into a memory-of-the-present, a present
imperceptibly gone by, a present almost past. By force of the
prosaic, music becomes language again. Tolstoy himself has
proven that distance is necessary, that it is impossible to be
consistent with the true.

And besides, does it follow that if music is incapable of
expressing ideas, or even emotions, it would nonetheless be
able to describe landscapes, narrate events, or imitate the
sound of nature?

VIOLENCE

Giving up expression: this does not always happen without a
fight. The need for expression entails a will to repression. The
result of this—a conflict between the vehemence of the expressionist instinct and the rigor of the censorship that suppresses it—is sheer violence, wrathful terrorism that withdraws at once from the sonorous gentleness of impressionist
harmony and the orgies of expressionist incontinence: this
terrorism is passionately antihedonist. How should violence
not be profoundly ambivalent? This hypermodern violence,

ich is not afraid to injure itself, is literally a phobia about
pression. That is to say that expression, for our impassioned
odernism, is simultaneously a temptation and an object of
horror. Expression—that which addresses itself to others,
looks with friendship into our eyes, and bears meaning—
expression as allocution becomes a kind of taboo.

Expression is at once determination and allocution, and it
is by no means coincidental that the word *expression* also applies to the human face, the part of the human form that is
the most significant and communicative, the most individu-
alized and determined. The shifting traits on a human face are
a site of tenuous signs and intentions, signs of intelligence or
tacit agreement, of sympathy and antipathy; and moreover the
human form, a sacred image of divinity, expresses the human
person's inimitable singularity, his or her incomparable "ipseity" and precious semelfactivity (as an "occurrence" that
happens "only once") in a extraordinarily precise way. "The
world aspires constantly to figure itself";[27] proceeds constantly
from the equivocal and amorphous to univocal meaning, to
luminous form, toward the fine and monadic truth of the
"hapax." Groping in the shadows of confusion and the nebulousness of chaos, the inchoate tends toward beauty, *forma
formosa*, the accomplishing of form.

Violence, however, cuts communications with other people
and massacres determinants that are nonetheless constantly
being reborn: in this, violence is a bit sacrilegious and a bit
masochistic. Violence tries desperately to do away with phys-
iognomic expressiveness and furthermore delights in tortur-
ing tonality, in executing tonality along with intonation and
all the other expressive determinants in song.

The means are many. There is the cruel rictus, the ugly
grimace that shrinks a face into a sad contraction of its basic
elements. In breaking a supple or graceful arabesque, in making a discontinuous or angular line out of a curve, they transform "ipseity" into an impersonal thing, into the anonymous

or the leaderless. The malicious grin is closed off; it refuses dialogue. There is atrocious dissonance, the sharp will toward ugliness, antihedonism, taking up the cause of indeterminism by ignoring all the benchmarks that attract the ear as well as all recognizable polarities: the familiar points of reference are hunted down without mercy whenever and wherever they crop up.

Nonetheless, it is important to distinguish here between destructive violence and inspired violence. The former, lacking any immediate point as it does any passionate conviction, stamps its feet, desperately, to conceal its own incurable aridity. But with Stravinsky, Bartók, Prokofiev, and Milhaud, violence is, on the contrary, fundamental. *Vociferation*: this is the word written at the head of the first chorus in Milhaud's *Choréophores*. The wild cry, at the very moment that it is contorting the face, is mistreating and brutalizing the melodic line: thus it is expressive *music* that is being bullied, manhandled, and furiously trampled to death. Subject to the blasphemies and catcalls of violence, music assumes the implacable aspect of an *Allegro barbaro*, *Scherzo barbaro*, *Sonata barbara*. Bartók's *Sonata barbara* for piano, brutal, far from meditative, is in its own way a *Pas d'acier*, a movement in steel, like Prokofiev's ballet. Darius Milhaud writes the words "dry and muscular" at the beginning of his first *Rag-Caprice*. Wrong notes, aggressive, provocative wrong notes shriek and laugh maliciously in Prokofiev's five *Sarcasms*. The rudeness of the discourse expresses, with supreme eloquence, the disdain felt by all these composers for the well-turned phrase, for melodic grace or academic elegance. Violence crucifies form.

But if violence as debilitation creates deformity—deformed form—then violence as inspiration reverts to the inchoate, which is the source of all forms. For form, persecuted and maligned, will reform itself in infinity: with truly brilliant composers, the massacre of determination, far from being purely destructive, is the foundation for a new, unique beauty.

Milhaud's polytonality, Stravinsky's violence, or Prokofiev's or Bartók's, and the forceful dynamism of certain works by Tansman, Martinů's rarely flagging energy: these things "express" something once more. The twentieth century's sturdy blasphemers discovered the source of a strange poetry, a more refined sort of musical delight.

EXPRESSING NOTHING WHATSOEVER. AFFECTED INDIFFERENCE

Yet violence is perhaps not the most effective way to strangle expression: since there is in its very furor, in its outrage, something suspect that betrays the passionate intention, torment and humanity, and an all-too-human anguish. The wrenching cry heard here and there in Ravel's music: is this not the most unmediated expression of pain and terror?[28] It is as if music, having arrived at an extreme of objectivity, rediscovered the Appassionata that it had disowned, as if the musician were expressing himself in the very act of not wanting to do so. Apart from silence, where music annuls itself, we can distinguish different degrees of inexpressive expression: Nothing at All; the Opposite or Something Else; Less; in General; Afterthought. Such would be the different degrees among our contemporaries.

Wishing not to express oneself is the great coquetry of the twentieth century. If the *grimace* is the sad result of violence,[29] the *mask*, as much abstraction as absence, is the immobilized face of inexpressiveness. Torture, distorting one's features, forces one's facial expression into a grimace, but the mask immobilizes the grimace. The malicious grin is frozen; the rictus finally congeals; the mask imposes rigid features upon the mobile and variable features of a living human being. For what is an immutable expression—that is, an expression free from the vicissitudes and affective oscillations of the humoresque—if not the degree zero of nonexpression? It is not at

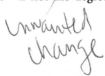

the nadir of the *Disperato* that joyousness rebounds? Expression is not expressive—as with Liszt, Chopin, Schumann, or Chaikovsky—except through changes in mood, through the alternation between elegy and joy or depression and exaltation, where the diurnal and the nocturnal are corollaries. The mask effaces the antithesis of Friska and Lassù;[30] it flattens the great spaces between the separate contours of tragedy and comedy, and it immobilizes contrast—which is the fundamental rhythm, the very source of breath of the life of the emotions. It makes contrast uniform. In a human being, a perpetual smile would become a horrifying grimace. By "eternalizing" a present instant, art accomplishes the miracle of the smile that is always smiling, like the one hovering on the lips of the Mona Lisa.[31] Masks fossilize the rainbow of expressions at the same time as they petrify animation in a cyclone of unstable emotions. *Masques:* the title Debussy gives to a dance whose allure is a little mechanical and stationary, where the obstinacy and monotony of the rhythm hinders all development. Satie's mechanical objects, Séverac's barrel-organs, Ravel's automata and clocks, the puppets in Stravinsky and Falla, the noise of the machines in Prokofiev, all reveal the same phobia concerning lyric exaltation or pathetic élan. Mechanical pianos and mechanical birds, scornful marionettes and wound-up automatons: all this artificial music, as a sacrilegious counterfeit, waxes ironic about the Appassionato, its tenderness and its languor.

To a certain extent, the modernist bestiary is a response to the same distrust: with their stammers, their tics and rambling nonsense, the animals of Satie or Ravel make a monkey house out of human passion. Trotted out over and over again, the cacophony of foxes, vixens, toads, and frogs in *The Cunning Little Vixen* is one of the forms of antirhetoric characteristic of Janáček's genius, as of Musorgsky's. The monotonous lament of the animals, the metallic clicking of the beetles, the cuckoo's two notes: do they not evoke a sort of derisory humanity, an automaton humanity midway between the human being and the pendulum? We can assemble Bartók's titles and say that modern music is not just the *Allegro barbaro* but also the *Marcia delle bestie*, the diary kept by a fly.[32]

The phobia about the sostenuto pedal, the suspicions about *rallentando* and *rubato*, these phobias and mistrusts (already so evident in Gabriel Fauré's pianism) are doubtless translations of a similar scruple with regard to pathos: dissipating the pedal's vapors denudes and desiccates the musical writing; burlesque staccatos then force it to wince. In Liszt, Chopin, or Scriabin,[33] the Burla wants to be bizarre and demonic, but the modernist Burla seeks buffoonery: Choute has dethroned Mephistopheles. In Prokofiev's op. 12, the four bassoons create a kind of burlesque concert that coughs and huffs and grins maliciously among the low notes. The sarcastic Burla, in Prokofiev and Alexandre Tansman,[34] has sharp pizzicati that prick pinholes in the gently shaded-off mist of musical impressionism, just as Picasso's angular lines and wicked dots prick the vagueness, the subtle gradation of color and the cottony fog that drowns Monet's countryside or Carrière's portraits. Dry jabs riddle a mocking scherzo. The scherzo's pointillism, which jabs a single note in a discontinuous instant, is the art of brushing lightly.

This sense of touch, is it not an imponderable and impalpable form of tangency? The staccato (in the realm of the temporal), like brachylogy (in the realm of development), relates to a phobia about the pathos of lingering. Satie's little pieces are perhaps no more than a kind of extended pizzicato. The scherzo forbids vibration, which is the source of the almost-there, of continuity, that which prolongs previous sounds into the next ones, and, in realizing the fusion of past and present, the past's survival or resonance within the present, in a word, creates the immanence that we call "Becoming." And in the same way, the rule of the metronome knows no pity and

curbs the frenetic accelerando of the Friska, prohibits the
ritardando that softens and slows too-passionate tempos, and
creates languor. The prohibition against ritardando means
that implacable chronometrics must cast out all weakness and
ignore human lassitude. Acceleration and deceleration: are
they not symptoms of the Fantasy, the Ballade, and the Rhap-
sody? A chronometer stops abruptly, without adagios or reveries, when its spring winds down. A motor never feels sorry
for itself. An automaton has no knowledge of the irregularities
and inequalities that result from the caprices of human nature. Don't be late; keep walking. Don't rush, but above all,
don't slow down, for someone might believe that your heart
has been moved. With Milhaud and Poulenc, this affectation
of apathy and imperturbability becomes a point of honor, as
if it were the consequence of a private wager.

In condemning pedaling and ritardando, inexpressive music on the one hand condemns insistence, on the other, complacency: it prevents the sound from being heard beyond the
moment when it is struck, imposing on discourse the uniform
speed of the machine. In a word, it liquidates *nuance*: the
infinitesimal variations of timbre and intensity, the delicate
inflections that sonority owes to the attack and to touch, impressionist pianissimo, Romantic crescendo. None of these are
its business. Contact has been broken between the vibrating
matter and the nerve endings of the supersensitive human
agent. Fauvism ignores the qualitative subtleties of half tones;
and in Bartók, there is no room for the shadings, reflections,
and exquisite transparencies of Debussyism. No more blue
shadows "in the ecstasy of a rose-gray moon"[35]—instead, brutal colors that shriek when they find themselves together.

If Fauré might seem the Verlaine of music (at least for a
moment), then Prokofiev would be more it's Myaskovsky.
Hence the *style plat*, the flat style that is imposed upon Satie's
music by irony, hermeticism, and hieraticism, notably in *Socrate*, the imperturbable cantata, in which music carefully

avoids seeming to have any relationship whatsoever to the words. Music seems to accept not taking account of Plato's text as its duty: for, just as the *Phaedo* conjures away the tragedy of death, so Satie's psalmody smooths out incidents in the Platonic narrative. In Ravel's *Chansons madécasses*, song seems at times oddly indifferent to the passionate words the singing voice declaims. "Indifferent." "Without nuance."

Such performance directions, destined to repress the Appassionata's human temptations, or curb the easy effect like crescendo, create a mask that cannot be breached, not just for Maurice Ravel's *Sainte* or *Le Gibet* or the "Estampe" that Debussy entitled *Pagode*, but also for the most tender of Mompous's works, or those of Milhaud, or Poulenc.[36]

THE OPPOSITE, SOMETHING ELSE, LESS.
HUMOR, ALLUSION, AND UNDERSTATEMENT

"I'm longing to say the most profound words to you: I don't dare. I fear your laughter. That's why I mock myself, and drown out my secret in jests . . . I'm longing to say the most sincere words to you: I don't dare. That is why I disguise them as lies, saying the opposite of what I think."[37] The words seem as if written expressly for Gabriel Fauré, the Fauré who wrote *Secret* and *Don silencieux*. Something, however, tells us that this coolness might well be an alibi and that there is a good measure of affectation in such indifference. The mask, acting as a pseudophysiognomic double for a real and changing physiognomy, does the mask not hide vehement emotions?

Music does not conceal meaning in order to reveal it: that is the strategy of coquetry. Rather, it reveals the meaning of meaning: music reveals the meaning of meaning in concealing it, and vice versa renders this meaning volatile and fugitive in the very act by which it reveals it. One could say the same of music that Heraclitus of Ephesus said of the Oracle of Delphi: (μαντεῖον) οὔτε λέγει οὔτε κρύπτει, ἀλλὰ σημαίνει; (the oracle) neither speaks nor conceals, but rather, gives signs. It is not difficult to tumble to the fact that inexpressive music is a tactic, a feinting motion: this unfeeling person, like the secretly passionate ironist, is simply *pretending.* The gentler he is, the more he will adopt an opaque manner; he loves to appear hard.

This is Ravel, inscrutable, writing the words "without expression" under the phrase in *Le Gibet* most suffused with pathos, or Eric Satie, in the *Morceaux au forme de poire*, prescribing the need to play "like an animal" at the place where the pianist encounters music that is tender and moving to the extreme. Malicious teasing or cruel ambivalence? There is something irritating in so ferociously ascetic a position, which contradicts the human heart's most natural tendencies: the rigors of the prohibition appear to increase in proportion to the strength of the temptation. In *Le Tombeau de Couperin,* expressing himself *a contrario,* Ravel composes five serene, smiling dances for five friends killed in the war. A musician who expresses himself this way, in reverse, is also confiding in us, but in an indirect or oblique way, which one must interpret counterintuitively.

Sometimes music does not express "the opposite" but "something else." This is the function of humor and the puzzling ruse in Satie. Humor is always good as an excuse: it is the alibi and the pretext that allows one to say serious things in play, in short, a way of being serious without seeming to, rather as irony serves to convey great truths under the guise of smoke and jesting. Déodat de Séverac, speaking of *"Toto déguisé en suisse d'église,"* raises himself to the grandiose.[38] Indirectly, secondarily, or ironically, an oblique modesty is being expressed via Satie's mystification and incognitos. Let us talk, if you don't mind, about Something Else: for instance, about Charles X, or the Battle of Cimbres, about the American frog, or Pantagruel's childhood.

Better still: perhaps all of music is in essence allegory and alibi—since a succession of sounds is, in itself, something entirely different from an emotion. If spoken words do not resemble in any way the emotion that they express, there is a compelling reason to imagine that a "suggestive" melody might not resemble in any way the emotion it suggests. If a man whose heart has been moved sings, his singing is of an entirely different order than his joy (or sadness), just as acoustic vibrations are of an entirely different order than psychological facts. *Not revealing readily; hesitant*

The mark of reticence is not solely that one speaks about *something else*, but also, and above all, that one says *less* about it, and with "less" one must understand not a simple quantitative diminution, or an attenuation of intensity, but a certain intentional and spiritual aspect of the discourse itself. The spirit of understatement is that of a human being who is no longer secretive, but discreet: reproaching in him- or herself the expressive fury of the Apassionato and the Disperato, remaining in a constant state of withdrawal with regard to emotion. On could say that for Stravinsky, Roussel, Maurice Emmanuel, Koechlin, Satie, Fauré, and even Saint-Saens, Hellenism served in this regard as a school for frugality, the effective antidote to nocturnal expressionism and the romantic Apassionato. Satie's music, like Socrates in the *Phaedo*, is careful to avoid all excess, πλημμελεῖν (to play a false note), and invites those who listen to restrain their sobs, καὶ ἡμεῖς ἀκούσαντες ᾐσχύνθημέν τε καὶ ἐπέσχομεν τοῦ δακρύειν,[39] to practice walking in bare feet, or in poverty's rude sandals.

To look for the half-light, paint in half-tones, half-say, with a lowered voice: in all these forms of allusion and of continence, a quasi-ascetic will shows through, the will to arrest oneself in mid-flight on the way to exaggeration. *En sourdine*: muted. With Fauré, the spirit of the mute, if not always the soft pedal itself, cushions and sifts the flashes of passion, the frenetic crescendo, the escalation, exaggeration of pathos.

Chapter
Two

48

outer shadow

Emotions "in a penumbra"[40] do not express themselves in capital letters. Interrupted inflation is the Fauréian regime par excellence, just as the "interrupted serenade" is that of Debussy. In Fauré's *Requiem*, in the Offertorium in which deflation constantly trumps inflation, the wave rises and falls in alternation. The understatement that reins in crescendos also cuts pedal points short: truly it was for a joke that Déodat de Séverac invented the "short pedal point," the notational sign that says to the pianist, "Do not fall asleep, do not get too sentimental."

With passionate composers, the final chord resonates and lingers and extinguishes itself with complacency in the aureole of an apotheosis that is both moribund and interminable. The spirit of understatement shortens that glorious agony, and wakes us from ecstasy, conjures away the gradations of the pedal point. Sometimes a curt pirouette,[41] preventing sonority from playing the professional beauty and lounging around in a cloud of pedal, suggests that the confidence being made need not be taken so seriously. The scherzo's humor, the humor of pizzicatos, cuts short the dying effusion by means of reticence. More generally, it is humor that shortens the development, strangles the indiscreet romance: the Interrupted Serenade, as if to abash us, represses the temptation toward constantly reborn eloquence, arrests it in mid-flight: it is thus that Platonic dialectics turns an ironic eye upon Protagorus's sophist discourse and the orators' tirades. Chaikovsky suspends his reverie only to roll out his Venetian romance,[42] but the Interrupted Serenade, with Debussy as with Musorgsky, submits to a true exercise is ascetics: because Debussy's ninth piano prelude is really interrupted, just as Albeniz's *El Albaicin* is an interrupted serenade.

But what am I saying? All of Debussy's piano preludes are more or less interrupted serenades, interrupted tarantellas (*Les collines d'Anacapri*), interrupted habaneras (*La puerta del vino, Iberia*), the interrupted cantilena of the oboe in *Gigues*—

*perf.
chapter*

these are other instances of the same ascetics. We read at the end of "Asie" in *Shéhérazade*, that it is a matter of "interrupting the tale artfully." And Ravel's *L'Heure espagnol* is one long succession of interrupted serenades. With all these composers, the fear of abusing their own compositional facility is immense.

Brachylogy is the most natural form of understatement: Ravel, criticizing Mahler's symphonic immensities, makes a laughing stock of all that indecent and loquacious sincerity, the progenitor of indiscreet confidences, intimate journals, and wordy autobiographies. The laconic impulse of the *Pièces brèves*, for Fauré, expresses a need for density and sobriety. Is implication not a prolonged pièce brève, the aura of reticence that augments brevity? The arid and sparing concision of a Ravel, the austerity of a Falla, the heroic held-back quality of a Debussy: these are lessons in reticence and sobriety for those suffering from affective exhibitionism and musical incontinence.

Understatement proves the independence of quality in relation to quantity, and makes manifest, paradoxically, the expressive effectiveness of contained expression: the inexpressive, and a fortiori the least expression, suggest meanings, and do so more powerfully than complete, direct expression. Just as "better" is the enemy of "well," thus "too much" guarantees its dialectical defeat. It is a commonplace: it is not by saying "everything" that one explains oneself best. Satie's *Socrate* bears witness to the sovereign force of reticence, the force of shielded emotion, which owes nothing to wild gesticulation. One recognizes the depth of emotion that understatement can attain in Fauré, the force of evocation it can summon in Debussy, for the superlative is usually weaker than the positive. True eloquence mocks eloquence's adjectival excess. Modesty about one's own artistic facility, about reactions too long awaited, reticence about tears and verbal exaggerations, reticence in the face of all detestable verbosity: the spirit of understatement reins in the extremist temptations that slum-

Concise writing speech?

few words

Chapter
Two

50

ber in all human beings. The spirit of understatement regulating mechanism that contains frenzy.

TO DESCRIBE, TO EVOKE, TO RECOUNT ALONG ROUGH LINES

Contemporary music is not just jealously guarded vis-à-vis expression of feelings but discreetly allusive as well in its description and representation of things. Impressionist objectivity—in which I have not tried to see anything besides a form of reticence, a phobia about confidences—is, itself, discreetly evasive, idealist, and non-realist. Landscape, in Debussy's Preludes, serves as diversion from outpourings of intimacy, but in turn this landscape is itself a kind of spiritual state. Debussyan clouds, for Paul Dukas,[43] appear as if "reduced to an imponderable state" and vaporized in the ether: by means of an allusive transposition, imitation has become the analogy of an analogy and the symbol of a symbol. *Évocation*:[44] Albeniz's title takes the twelve flamboyant "impressions" in *Iberia* and envelops them in advance in the sea mists of memory and the unreal. With Liszt, Novák, Josef Suk, Myaskovsky, Alexandrov, Prokofiev, and Albeniz, there is significantly more than a *Ricordanza*. In *Adieux à la jeunesse* (a popular melody in lower Brittany harmonized by Bourgault-Ducoudray), music exhales the sweet melancholia of irreversibility and regret about the years that have fled into the past. The "pastness" of the past: is it not a charm, or an unknowable something whose indeterminate expression is music? *Pour évoquer l'image du passé*: the melancholy arpeggios that constitute Mompou's fifth "Charme" have this express purpose. Anatoly Alexandrov's first *Vision* also displays the "depths of memory." For the past, absence and its languor, the nostalgia of reminiscence, furnish music with a distant milieu, the place where music is hiding its messages.[45] The third symphony of Rachmaninoff: is it not through and through a poem about exile and nostalgia? Albeniz's *Evocation*: not a Spain seen from far away, seen by an exile? In Aleksey Nikolayevich Tolstoy's *Dekabristï* (*The Decembrists*), one of the heroes, hearing the bells of Moscow, says, "Nothing brings back the past so well as sounds."

Even more than descriptive music in general, melody in particular reveals that musical expression has a diffluent nature. Music does not "explain" word by word, nor does it signify point by point; rather, it suggests in rough terms, not being made for line-by-line translation or for the reception of indiscreet intimacies, but rather for atmospheres, spiritual evocations. In a melody by Fauré, music's relation to text, far from being a relationship defined by strict parallelism, appears as an indirect or very general rapport: a simple ensemble effect.

In this relationship, necessary but insufficient, with its material substrate, one can see to a certain extent the very ambiguity that characterizes "cerebration." The brain is a general condition for memory, in the sense that there is no memory without a brain—and nonetheless memories do not divide up, neuron by neuron, in the different folds of the brain's surface. Soul, thought, life, and individual presence are inherent in the existence of a body in general—and nonetheless the soul cannot be pinpointed here or there in the body: the soul is not localizable, but more a diffuse presence, like the grace that (according to Plotinus) is scattered everywhere to array beauty in the form in which it is perceptible to the senses, χάρις ἐπιθέουσα τῷ κάλλει, "grace playing upon beauty."[46] The soul, which exudes carnal presence in general like a perfume and nonetheless evades all topographies, the fugitive, ambiguous soul: is it not a kind of Charm? The soul is the Charm engendered by the body.

This ubiquity, this everywhere and nowhere exclusive of a somewhere, this omnipresent presence that is at the same time omniabsence, also characterizes the present absence of

meaning in a sentence, and of the Charm in music. If the
meaning of a sentence is inherent in the totality of that sentence, without any of the fragments of the sentence necessarily
corresponding to fragments of that "meaning," if a fortiori a
poetic verse's Charm—which is the meaning of a meaning—
is inherent in the totality of this verse and the meaning of this
verse, then music—the "charm of the Charm"—will emanate
like an evasive meaning from the totality of the poem. Words
and signs draw together or dislodge one another like bits of
parquetry, but meaning itself does not fragment—in this, it
bears a resemblance to freedom. Meaning does not fragment,
and nonetheless meaning can be analyzed according to groups
of phrases, by single phrases or even clauses. As for the meaning of the meaning—the Charm—it is always total; that is, it
exists, or does not; it is not a total equal to the sum of its
parts but an indivisible and impalpable totality such that displacing one syllable is enough to cause something qualitative
to fade away. Dissection, applied to the anatomy of the charm,
will produce nothing more that frightful, miserable disjecta.
Music, the "charm of the Charm" does not even have need of
a verbal body to express, if not meaning, then at least a directed intention, since music without a literary component is
not lost, wandering music, not at all.

All the same, music (as in Fauré) brings out what the poem
signifies (even though it would be able to live without the
poem), or, rather, transposes this signification according to
other designs entirely, into another environment entirely. Music makes the poem its environment, drinks up all its syllables,
impregnates them to the point of silence—and has no need to
spell them out note by note and word by word; and as a result
fragments of music do not at all correspond to fragments of
poetry. Thus the melody of Fauré's *En sourdine* is coextensive
with Verlaine's poem and nevertheless does not tangle itself
up in the details of the text, preferring rather to drown them
in the unvarying pianissimo of the arpeggios, in the penum-

bra, in the end taking no account of the nightingale's singing. If it is true that one hears the swallow's chirps in *La Bonne chanson*, one will nonetheless also observe that, in setting the *Chanson d'Ève*, Fauré was careful not to choose the "Poème de sons" with its clear invitation to onomatopoieia.

Satie's *Socrate* itself never yields to the narrative's dramatism, does not follow all the anecdotal zigzags and makes no slavish translation of incident; when solicited by the text to take note, it simply ignores that request. And, nonetheless, Satie's music is, somehow, "present" to Plato's text, present, omnipresent in its serene equanimity. In melodrama—declamation accompanied by orchestra, an intermediary genre between sung ballad and symphonic poem—the *melos* and the *drama* are at no point in counterpoint to one another; the music is a sonic background under the poem and does not follow the poem's recitation verse by verse; it creates a general climate, a shifting background that evolves less continuously, less progressively than a melody, and it is also less voluble than poetry. Such is the case in Liszt's melodrama *Lenore*.[47]

What has just been said about poems, librettos, and texts in melodrama could be resaid about the "programs" in Liszt: do not try to find Orpheus's starry robe, or the rapt lions, or Eurydice's rescue—all the things announced in the preface—in the music of *Orpheus*. And nonetheless the music as a whole gives voice to a triumph, the ascendancy of civilizing Harmony, albeit in another form entirely, in a nondiscursive form.

And, finally, what is true of program music is true of "narrative" music and "biographical" music: music is no more narrative than it is discursive. Just as it does not draw consequences from an idea, music cannot narrate strictly speaking, cannot "recount" the stages of a promenade or the episodes in a life. Several piano pieces by Nicolas Medtner and by Prokofiev have the title *Skazka*, "Story."[48] But what do they recount? Even the most rhapsodic poems by the great Russian composers, even the most descriptive pages in *Pictures at an Exhibition* retain an indefinable indeterminacy.

This is no less true of Richard Strauss: hearing the *Alpensymphonie*, no one who does not see the score and its markings could know that Strauss is "narrating" an ascent "in music," that this ascent begins at dawn, goes through a forest, then along a stream, then a waterfall, and at last (after having cleared a glacier) ends in the summit, where a vertiginous panorama is discovered; that a storm then surprises our mountain climber; and that all ends as it had begun, in darkness. The two nights that enclose the summer day on the mountain thus project the form of a circle onto the music, a circle of shadow, making it—at its extremes—twilight music. And this is even less true of Debussy who, in the first part of *La mer*, "De l'aube à midi sur la mer," follows the sun's course from the mists of dawn to the meridinal splendors of its zenith. Debussy does not narrate events from the ocean's daily levee: because this half-day is as much static as agitated, as empty of events as it is full of wind. "Biographical" music, "Journals," and "Hero's Lives" have not been lacking in music history. Max Reger and Richard Strauss are nevertheless no threat to novelists: *Aus meinem Tagebuch,* Don Quixote's adventures, Don Juan's serial erotic involvements, Till Eulenspiegel's merry pranks remain, despite the instrumental picturesque, in the vague realm of approximation and imprecision.

Liszt, dedicating a symphonic poem to the life of Tasso, does not narrate the successive events that constitute its fabric: what music could be "narrative" in this sense? Instead, he detaches certain characteristic episodes from that life: the gondolier's singing in the Venetian lagoon; a persucuted Torquato Tasso haunting the Ferrarese court; the poet's apotheosis in Rome. And this, the panorama, simplified, is itself reduced to a diptych—the diptych of Lamento and Trionfo: Tasso in prison; Tasso's posthumous glory; "Death and Transfiguration," an antithesis that summarizes poets' destinies in general. "Three Characteristic Images": that is all that is kept of *Faust* in the Faust Symphony, the picturesque episodes. For instance, in part II, Marguerite plucking petals from the daisy, to find out whether she is loved or not; the devil's sarcasm, and his faint limp, in part III; in part I, the naive choruses celebrating the Nativity: all these details fade out, become blurred and vague; anecdotes, reduced to the state of attenuated suggestions, evasions, originating in the depths of a wholly subjective tragedy. In *Les Préludes*, Liszt (following Lamartine) evokes four exemplary scenes, four typical aspects of human destiny: love, the storms of being, pastoral life, war. More diffluent and more austere, the triptych *Du berceau à la tombe* evokes—apart from and other than the "struggle for existence"—the lullaby for a child, and the lullaby of death, for human beings, waking up in the afterlife, close the cycle of destiny. Without abstract schemes or futile stylization, the lives of all creatures and the human condition in general are here expressed in their naked essence.

Smetana's marvelous Quartet in E minor ("Z mého života") does not trace a life as it evolves continuously from year to year, or the course of this evolution; rather, it chooses four significant signposts across the many ages of that life and summarizes their drama: the artist's aspiration toward an ideal that cannot be expressed; Bohemian polkas (evoking Smetana's sunny childhood); love, as dreamy and melancholy as the past itself; finally, the bearer of ill tidings, the high, piercing E, the sign, the remorseless advance runner of affliction, announces the composer's deafness. These four stages emerge as if from the damp wind of a dream; they restore and refresh a certain continuity of atmosphere in the same way that Debussy's scattered musical notation, his discontinuous sevenths, nonetheless project a continuous, luminous aura.

This autobiography—if autobiography there is—is a bit dream-like: it conveys the "meaning of a meaning," that is, the meaning along with that which has revealed it, the secondary meaning, and it hides the primary meaning, the meaning that is in short absurd (because it is a mixture of sense and nonsense)—the very meaning of life cut off by death, and nonetheless superior to death. Someone lived, suffered, hoped, and—with all the strength he could muster—sought "nonexistent things," the same nonexistent things that Fauré has in his sights. There is no conclusion to be made, but one wishes (like the prisoner of Mons) to interrogate one's soul: "tell me, you there, what did you make of your childhood?" No. Unlike a writer's diary, a sonata is not circumstantial, not done in detail.

Music signifies something in general without ever wanting to say anything in particular. *Mouvement*: in this "Image" for piano, Debussy evokes movement as a general thing, the pure undetermined essence of mobility, whether the moving object is a breathless runner, or a dead leaf being chased by the wind, or a top spinning in place; the whirling triplets tell of circular motion, in the abstract. And this is true as well not only when music is expressing a meaning it claims to suggest to us but also when it expresses emotion, an emotion that it succeeds in inspiring within us. For the expression of feeling in Fauré is as indeterminate as Debussy's description of landscapes. Etienne Souriau has described the first of these phenomenons as "abstraction of feeling," and Bayer in turn speaks of a "generalizing sensibility" that aspires to the "essence of feelings."[49] Such feelings, always a bit generic, are what music is supposed to be able to translate. Fauré calls one of his *Pièces brèves* "Allégresse," "Happiness":[50] the C major arpeggios, arpeggios with wings, flying from one end of the white keys to another, express unmotivated joy, indeterminate joy without a cause. In a piece from *Dolly* called "Tendresse," the two pianists conduct a canonic dialogue without exchanging precise ideas: this could be the soul, silent, conducting a monologue with itself.

No less vague is the nostalgia that Fauré expresses in setting Théophile Gautier, in the melody for *Tristesse*. Scriabin's *Désir* is a piece where premonitions babble, languor is exhaled, impetus is repressed, and aspiration overlaps with who-knows-what. With Poulenc, *Melancholie* is an album-leaf, hardly sad, in D-flat major: its gentle animation, its resistance to the Ritardando, seems to waver between passion and humor.[51] The three *Vzpomínky* (Reminiscences) of Vítězslav Novák— *Triste, Inquieto, Amoroso*—or Josef Suk's *Un poco triste* (op. 17, no. 3), similarly express emotions without causes. The Lisztian Disperato, is it not despair in existing, in general, a despair without ascribable tragic cause? Music is—and this is deeply paradoxical—the realm of "qualitative abstraction," or, if one can put it this way, of concrete schematicism. Schopenhauer said (correctly, and with great insight) that music does not express this determined state of joy or that particular sadness, but instills in us Melancholy in general, Joy in general, Serenity itself, Hope without a cause. Nietzsche goes further still:[52] music does not even express sadnesss-in-general, or joy-in-general but rather indeterminate Emotion, the pure emotional force of the soul: music exalts the faculty of feeling, an abstraction assembled from all feelings that qualify, whether Regret, Love, or Hope: music awakens in us affect per se, affect that is unspecified and unmotivated. Those who deal with music as a medium to express certain determinate emotions remain "in the forecourt" (thus Nietzsche), without having access to the sancta sanctorum.

Nietzsche doubtlessly passes a little too quickly over the specificity of affective essences awakened by music; there is really no way to mistake the mad jubilation of *Eritana* (Albeniz) for the nostalgia exuded by Liszt's *Heimweh*. But it is no less the truth that from the semantic point of view, as a "language" of emotions, music remains equivocal and disappointing, always. Always signifying in general and never in particular, music is the domain where ambiguity holds sway.

Thus, too, are the soul, liberty, life: evident in the totality and as an effect of mass, but always given lie to, in each individual point that might be contested, in every detail. Music does not express any meaning that can be assigned to it—and none-theless, music is, *grosso modo*, expressive, powerfully so. In-capable of developing, inept when it comes to any discursive unfolding, how would music express itself, if not along rough lines?

TO SUGGEST IN RETROSPECT

In songs, and in symphonic poems with programs, a meaning comes first, and music brings out secondarily the meaning of that meaning. Now, it can also be the case that the meaning of the meaning will emerge in retrospect, but directly, in pure music without pretexts. Liszt himself, though he announces all of his "programs" in advance, gets to the center, the soul and the heart, by some means other than his poets' poems: by means of an unimaginable, divine, troubling something, no-where present in Goethe's *Faust*, or Petrarch's sonnets, or Vic-tor Hugo's *Mazeppa*, but that *after all*, or *in summary*, will have explained the deepest essence of the literary text. In the same way Ravel, without knowing Spanish, will have given expression, better than Falla ever did, to Spain in its most intimate essence.

In Debussy's piano preludes, the meaning of the meaning expresses itself immediately on the basis of the music, just as the meaning of the meaning emerges secondarily from an an-ticipated, a priori meaning in program music (even though program music is not a "translation" of something into musi-cal language). Here, music is the intermediary between mean-ing and the "meaning of the meaning," between essence and quintessence, or between Meaning and the charm, charm that is exuded, without mediation, like a perfume. In Debussy's *Preludes*, famously, the titles are put at the end. Several works follow this example: Jacques Ibert's *Histoires*, Anatoly Alexandrov's *Visions*, Nikolay Myaskovsky's collection *Vospominaniya* (Reminiscences).[53] The decor is not imposed in advance, like a theme, but proposed retrospectively, only suggested.

In the same way, the meaning of a famous life, doubtful and left incomplete by the great man when he was alive, emerges in retrospect through the retroactive effect of death. In the same way, irregular, capricious, and discontinuous evolution in the moment reveals itself in retrospect as progressive: this evolution was the process of aging, undetectable while happening, but always verified at the end. Aging is the general meaning of our Becoming, even though it does not progress regularly, is not caused directly by the flight of days or the wearing effect of time.

Is this not the retroactive effect that Schelling calls *Erinnerung*? Here are some triplets that could be the scraps of a tarantella, dwindling away among unpredictable, unraveling rhythms and interrupted serenades: once silence has returned, Debussy makes us a suggestion—"Les Collines d'Anacapri"—but "Capriccio" could have served just as well. The suspended notes prolonging the dying vibration of the final pedal point, to the point of indeterminacy—they lend even more evasiveness, more atmosphere, to that which has been evoked. Anacapri is merely one setting among many, among hundreds of others that serve to narrow down ideas. Here, a habanera rhythm in all its passion, with violent alternations between piano and forte and arpeggios that seem like guitar figuration, sobbing guitars. And since habaneras evoke Madrid more than Naples, after the last chord has dies away one might as well say "La puerta del Vino," if you like.

But it goes without saying that the evasive tarantella and the very Parisian habanera in "Les collines d'Anacapri" could equally well have been entitled "Les fées sont d'exquises danseuses." Sometimes—as in "La Terrasse des audiences"—the suggestion made by the title is pure fantasy, so as to fetter as little as possible the performer's imagination. And it can even be the case that the title is involuntarily ambiguous: such is the ambiguity, the double meaning of music as the "charm of the Charm." This is the case with "Voiles," which suggests the fluttering of a veil over the water, but also—in that it follows "Danseuses de Delphes"—a veil undulating in the air: and who knows whether Debussy was not merely playing at equivocation in neglecting to dissipate that ambiguity?

Fauré prefers to leave the imagination wholly free and gives only the name of the keys as titles in his *Préludes*; and moreover, genre titles and abstract titles are used for his piano works in general. Unlike Fauré's unreal *Préludes*, Debussy's objective yet dream-like *Préludes* induce retrospective images in our minds as a result. But force of habit, of association and convention, will consolidate these fascinating suggestions, and end by making the plausible meaning proposed by the composer into something that is organically necessary and almost normative. No one can conceive of Chopin's second piano sonata in a key other than B-flat minor, or of Chopin's *Barcarolle* in a key other than F-sharp major; since the thirteenth Nocturne in C minor, that key has become elegiac a posteriori, just as B-flat major has become nocturnal since the *Berceuse* first appeared. In a similar way, finally, no one hearing certain electric tremolos, shudders or gruppettos or shafts of little notes, can now hear anything other than "Poissons d'or." In retrospect—after having been heard—music will assume its own, proper signification, and even its own metaphysics, even though it is never possible to determine what has been intended as meaning, unambiguously, in the breathless moment of hearing. Such is the finality of life, which Bergson says is always retrospective and never anticipated. This uncertainty, which precludes all foresight: it is not irritating? Musical meaning lends itself to the retrospective: music can only signify something in the future perfect tense: it "will have meant."

TO EXPRESS THE INEXPRESSIBLE INTO INFINITY

Music is, then, neither a "language," nor an instrumental means to convey concepts, nor a utilitarian mode of expression (since one is never required to sing); and yet music is not purely and simply inexpressive, since despite all this, the Espressivo is no sin. Robert Siohan, writing critically of the atonality and antithematic nature of much contemporary music, argues that music cannot be conceivable without an "intention": whether music is representational or not, *movement* and *quality* remain the sole guarantors of a human connection between music and audition.[54] Roland-Manuel, who has rehabilitated the arguments of Guy de Chabanon, discovers an "ars bene movendi" in music, independent of all ideation: music is not emotionally "moving" except in that it is literally "moving."[55]

Music lends itself willingly: in songs, it lends itself as translation of the poem; in opera, as a lyric commentary upon dramatic actions; in symphonic poems, in sacred music and program music, it is willing to illustrate a legend, liturgical or historical actions. But should "impure" music be deemed less musical that "pure" music? In effect, such "expressive" music is not musical *except* to the degree that it is never an unequivocal, unambiguous expression of a meaning.

Here, however, I should make a distinction between expression per se and "expression" as an element in interpretation. A single literary text lends itself to an infinity of radically unforeseeable musics; and the same music refers to an infinity of possible texts. Given a particular poem, it is impossible to predict the song that a composer will extract from it—for this is the secret of genius, its freedom, a secret far more mysterious than that of time yet-to-come and its potential novelty. How can one foresee the finale Borodin would have written had he finished his third symphony? And yet we sense that this finale, had it been written, would be at once absolutely

Borodin-like and absolutely different from anything we imagine, impossible to anticipate and yet allied to Borodin's artistic
genius by some sort of organic necessity. But it is no less
impossible, based on music already written, to reconstruct the
text or to divine the pretext that gave rise to that music: that
would be virtually impossible. Music, if a language, is a diffuse language, a general one, whose generality becomes partic-
ularized, in such a case, by what one already knows about its
subject or its author. To divine a musical setting based on a
literary text would be to place oneself at a crossroads where
innumerable possibilities meet. How did Fauré (op. 6, no. 3)
and Novák (op. 39, no. 5), with the same text by Verlaine,
end up with such different versions? Or Lalo and Liszt, with
same "Guitare" by Victor Hugo, or Balakirev ("Gruzinskaya
pesnya"), Rimsky-Korsakov (op. 51, no. 2), and Rachmaninoff
(op. 4, no. 4), with the same Pushkin poem? To divine the
source text through the music is to assign oneself a task where
there are nothing but unknowns, to grope indefinitely, hoping
for a miraculous accident: because in no case does interpretation duplicate the path taken by creation, nor can interpretation flawlessly reassemble (except by knowing the solution in
advance) an original intuition.

In effect, inexpressible nuances of disposition, the states of
mind and feelings, are as innumerable in the process of creation as are the musics to which they could give rise. How
would the performer—or the philosopher—in turn know
how to choose among the infinitude of qualitative nuances or
happen upon precisely that specific image or intuition—not
subject to articulation—that has given rise to this or that musical work? And more still: finding that it is standing before
infinity, possibility, and indeterminacy, the mind loses itself in
an inextricable crisscrossing of bifurcated bifurcation, in a
labyrinthine network of crossroads that branch into crossroads of crossroads. There are no more simple givens, but
rather complications that proliferate into infinity. The infi-

nitely equivocal: this is music's natural regime. The inexpressive Espressivo is first among its equivocations.

SERIOUS AND FRIVOLOUS, DEEP AND SUPERFICIAL. MUSICAL AMBIGUITY

How can one define the puzzling fact of inexpressive Expression, or expressive Inexpression, without letting oneself be trapped in antimony? No sooner does one discern a predicate than the opposite predicate reclaims its rights. For example: is music serious or not?

The answer can only be ambiguous. I showed how musical humor serves not to express, not at all, but more to suppress; moreover, how this impulse toward the alibi, toward expressing Something Else, is nonetheless whispering an indirect confidence in our ears. The comedian turns investigations aside, distracts attention from his own mystery; peppered with staccatos and speckled with pizzicatos, this comedian's humoresque is the art of brushing lightly without insisting and gliding without pressing down. If gravitas, in its self-importance, weighs heavily upon sound, winged pleasantries, on the contrary, fly over the piano without seeming to touch it. Music is humorous to the extent that it sends pathos packing.

But on the other hand, to the extent that the serious is a form of totality where comic indifference and tragic indifference cancel each other out, then music—unsuited to express precise sentiments, defined sentiments—is entirely serious: humor itself is serious in this sense. The Mendelssohnian scherzo, which is "humoresque," is serious in this same sense as his *Variations sérieuses*. The serious is not simply characteristic of legato as opposed to staccato, to the continuity of pathos as opposed to the discontinuity and pointillism of scherzo, not simply (as in César Franck) characteristic of a certain pure-music climate as opposed to the realm of frivolous imagery and the illustrators. Robert Siohan observes (along with Schopenhauer): it is music as a whole that avows itself incapable of translating, in itself or alone, incapable of suggesting with its own means anything like representative or superficial sentiments, such as comic sentiments.

The ridiculous in music arises only from associations that the mind forms secondarily with regard to the musical phrase. Musorgsky's *Rayok* (*The Peepshow*) would not engender laughter without the words that define a satiric intention. In themselves, in their pure musicality, that is to say separate from any literary imaginings, the puppets' tall tales in *Rayok* are no more tall tales than the drivel in *Seminarist* (*The Seminarist*) is drivel; in themselves, the detached, repeated notes in *Seminarist* are no more "amusing" than the tragic sonorities and funeral marches of *Pesni i plyaski smerti* (*The Songs and Dances of Death*). "Sous les lauriers roses" and "Recuerdos di mu rincon" make one smile based on little scenarios that Séverac on the one hand and Turina on the other have attached to their music, which end by rubbing off on that music. Without the texts that accompany them, what unsuspecting listener would sense buffoonery in this unintelligible musical unraveling, or sense only the humorous intention? It's a good bet that no one would notice a thing, not without cheating. In *Till Eulenspiegel*, the pizzicatos are of the order of farce, although in the *Faust Symphony*, the same pizzicatos are demonic sarcasm: but one must know the program to make the differentiation, and it is the writer who will decide between the trickster and the devil. Satie's humor in turn is not so much an audible phenomenon as an effect of the crazy verbal remarks scattered among the staves. Who knows whether operetta itself does not in fact always owe its comic effect to the libretto?

Music, as a vague and diffluent discourse, situates itself beyond discreet categories like comedy and tragedy: it is situated instead in the depths of lived existence itself. In Bartók, Pro-

kofiev, or Tansman, the musical "Burla" is the application of
comedy to tragedy. And can one say that music is, in its entirety, a game, or that it is entirely serious? Is this equivocal
position something it holds in common with poetry, theater,
or literature, with art in general, or not? Music is entirely
ludic in that it remains on the margins of any prosaic or utilitarian existence; and nonetheless, with regard to its immanent meaning, music is serious, absolutely serious, as distant
from comedy's fragmentation as from tragedy's engagement.
Frivolous? Not frivolous? It depends. Music represents more a
sort of "other Seriousness" a second kind of Seriousness,
paradoxically foreign to Seriousness pure and simple, that is,
foreign to the "real" Seriousness we associate with perception
and action.

In another way of speaking, music itself, and entirely, is a
kind of "fête," a celebration, and countless compositions have
titles that attest to its festival character: *Fêtes, Pour un fête de
printemps, Fête-Dieu à Seville, Svetlïy prazdnik, Festklänge.*[56]
But if the magical half-hour whose name is Sonata resembles
an enchanted oasis or a hidden garden in the desert expanse
of working days and business hours—an "isle heureuse" in
the quotidian ocean—this same half-hour, in that it becomes
an eternal present, a universe apart and a whole, is absolutely,
utterly serious.

In the same, way music is simultaneously "allegorical" and
(as Schelling said) "tautegorical." It is an allegory to the extent
that, through its reticence, it expresses by hinting, obliquely.
But if allegory is a detour taken by an express intention, or by
intentional expressionism, a system of ciphers or hieroglyphs
or ideograms, then music is, to the contrary, a "tautegory." To
the extent that music signifies something other, it is as suspect
as a painting done by numbers, as didactic poetry or symbolic
art: it is no longer music but ideology, a sermon meant to
edify. Considering its naive and immediate truth, music does
not signify anything other than what it is: music is not an

exposé, revealing some nontemporal truth; rather, it is exposition itself that is the only truth, the serious truth.

Such is the difference between the geometrist, the poet, and the flutist: the geometrist (like the Civil Code) says just what he has to say with regard to his proof, without innuendos or detours, without vocal ornaments, fioraturas, allusions—because trills and arpeggios are not the business of mathematicians. The poet says something else, a lot more or a lot less, but the very fact of amplifying or suggesting demonstrates that the poet's words already bear meaning. But as for the flutist, he is expressing absolutely nothing: his entire discourse is made of roulades and gestures. The very difference between phrase and paraphrase, between locution and circumlocution, between the song and the fioratura—the "blossom" of sound—undermines the dogmatic and pragmatic prejudice which insists that music, like language, must serve to transmit thoughts.

There is no space here to distinguish between substantive and circumstantial manners of being, between essence and ornament, where "lost time" itself is an ingredient of musical time, where cadences *senza tempo* and phalanxes of little notes may play a part in truth. Lost time, lost thought, lost efforts, lost life: is this not the paradox of poetry itself?[57] Now, it can happen that this lost time, like time spent strolling or walking aimlessly, can be time won back, time immediately rediscovered. Music's point, whether a prelude, an impromptu, or a sonata, is not to go a certain distance in the minimum of time required and arrive at a destination as quickly as possible, like some rushed functionary planning his itinerary according to the principle of maximum efficiency: in this case, singing is unnecessary. Music prefers the curved line to the straight line, which, as everyone knows, is the shortest distance between two points. Music prefers superfluous circular motions, notes for nothing: and even where music attains the most pointed state of concision, in Satie's or Mompou's tiny piece-lings, utilitarian anxiety about minimizing expenses counts for nothing in this brachylogy: to the contrary, such short pieces are elongated, prolonged, and made perennial by the reveries they suggest; their memory and their resonance survive long after the voice has been stilled. Futile perambulation, dawdling without a goal, musical discourse is velocity that slows itself down and that goes nowhere. And thus all is true or all is false, depending whether one grants melos the communicative function of logos or refuses to do so.

It is not (as Plato the antirhetorican has said) that there would be, strictly speaking, *paralipomenas*, παραλειπόμενα (literally, the left-out) in the fluteplayer's art, or fioraturas in the ode or the epic: in truth, it is music in its entirety that is a fioratura, a detour, an exquisite efflorescence of life itself; it is music in its entirety that (like the nightingale's ornaments) constitutes the luxurious, graceful paralipomena of practical existence.

All these ambiguities can be summarized as one: is the notion of depth applicable to music: yes *or* no? Once more, I need to answer in a noncommittal way: yes *and* no. As sonorous presence, music could be said to correspond, in its entirely, to the superficial actuality of the process of hearing it. In other words, music could occupy its phenomenal aspect, as appearance perceptible to the senses: in this initial sense, there would be nothing to look for behind the façade, no conclusion to be drawn, no consequence to deduce; the magic has a natural end, since it is its own meaning and raison d'être. Music, from this standpoint, is exactly what it appears to be, without secret intentions or ulterior motives. How could music harbor ulterior motives when it has no motives to begin with? Music decidedly does not acquire complexity and the false dimension of depth except by means of the musician's marginal speculations about it. As the pure sensation that is present in all performances, music does not say what it says, or better, does not "say" anything, to the extent that *to say* means to communicate a meaning. Music gives excellent ammunition to those who consider it mere insouciant play, or a frivolous diversion given over completely to the delights of appearance or inventive sensations. Ravel wrote some words by Henri de Régnier above the title of the *Valses nobles et sentimentales*: "the exquisite pleasure of a futile pursuit." Here, however, futility itself is produced by relinquishing all in favor of pure sensory evidentᵉness.

Music as a phenomenon of surfaces is nonetheless not alien to all forms of depth, although depth in this event would have no didactic or dialectic character. Music is certainly no system of ideas to be developed discursively, no truth that one must advance toward degree by degree, or whose implications must be explained, or whose import extracted, or whose far-reaching consequences must be made explicit. Yet despite everything, just as the richness of implicit and latent meaning slumbers within the words of a "deep" text, so a "deep" music accumulates within its notes—in a state of reciprocal implication—an infinite number of "virtualities"; just as the whole is immanent, according to Bergson, in each part, so the whole melody slumbers, enfolded, in each harmony. Thus, it can happen that hidden intentions at first pass unnoticed.

And on the other hand, in both these cases, the impression of depth is suggested to us by the very effort that will be necessary to delve into the intentions of the philosopher, or the musician, or better yet, will be suggested by the time required to actualize all that is virtual in the text or the musical work; depth, which is a spatial metaphor, is in short the projection of the time required for actualization. A phrase that is "heavy with meaning," for instance, is a phrase that seems a mere nothing but that "goes a long way," that initiates a long train of thoughts: a few words suffice to say it, and volumes would not suffice to explicate it, nor would an entire life suffice to contemplate it; depth is perhaps nothing more than that immense future time of reflection and perplexity wrapped within a few words in a simple phrase. Granted, these ﹍sibilities are not explicitly contained or conserved in each element of the phrase, or in each fragment of the melody, for it is the very unfolding of the discourse that causes them to crop up as things go along and that causes us to deem them immanent in retrospect. And the time required to digest a doctrine intellectually, to let it sink in, can be due to a debility of intellect: in this case, a mind blessed with limitless penetration would read intentions at a single glance, as if transparent, and in place of the most entangled complexities, will be granted a perfectly simple intuition. For an archangel, the *Faust Symphony* is as superficial as André Messager's *Les P'tites Michu*.

Music is an essentially temporal art, not a secondarily temporal one like poetry or dramatic literature or the novel. Of course, time is necessary to perform a play: but theatrical works can be read one right after the other, or in fragments, and in any order you please. A musical work does not exist except in the time of its playing. Now, this playing occupies a certain durational interval (by virtue of tempo), and one can work out its timing; the elapsed time is measurable but not compressible and would not submit either to being abridged or extended. Thus the sonata is properly speaking a succession of expressive contents that unfolds itself in time: it is an enchanted chronology, a melodious form of becoming, *time itself*. Sonata is sonorous time: the temporal realization of the virtualities contained in two musical themes. And it takes time for the listener to discover these virtualities and for the spirit to delve into the core of this immanence: there is a time for sinking in, and this time, perpendicular to the time of the performance (if one dares to use such language), is the time that the listener spends in delving into the thickness of this meaning devoid of meaning.

Time, first of all, is necessary if one is to grasp the musician's intentions, which went into constructing the piece, to recognize a theme within the variations that deform it to the

point of being unrecognizable, perceive all the allusions that
constitute the work's psychological context and ideological
circumference. And time is necessary, moreover, to familiarize
oneself with unfamiliar beauty, with harmonies that may be
alien to our habits of listening: so today's disagreeable simultaneity will become tomorrow's most refined form of pleasure. This test of time is the most sure criterion of "depth."
"Deep" music is like a rich essential nature in a human being:
one cannot appreciate the personality and the resources in the
first afternoon's encounter. No: it is not just due to an austerity complex or an antihedonistic mania that we suspect what
pleases us instantly. There is no unfathomable depth, but
there is an inexhaustible, unfailing, unflagging possibility of
emotion. In their resistance to seeming weary, in the permanent newness of great works, the miracle of eternal youth fulfills itself. In music, is repetition not often innovation?

The "depth" of the temporal work is, in short, another
name with which to designate reticence, the spirit that withholds and does not reveal all its resources at first or deliver up
the meaning of its meaning entirely, all at once. And since a
musical work itself performs itself, lets itself be heard along
the axis of time, it is hardly surprising that the richness of its
nonsignifying signification, or its inexpressive expressiveness,
is not flaunted in space, all at once, in its entirety, but unfolds
itself little by little, for patient, attentive ears: its depth calls
out to ours.

THE INEFFABLE AND THE UNTELLABLE.
THE MEANING OF MEANING

The mask, the inexpressive face that music assumes volun-
tarily these days, conceals a purpose: to *express infinitely that
which cannot be explained.* Music, said Debussy, is made for
that which cannot be expressed.[58] I will be more precise: the
mystery transmitted to us by music is not death's sterilizing

inexplicability but the fertile inexplicability of life, freedom, or love. In brief, the musical mystery is not "what cannot be spoken of," the untellable, but the *ineffable*. Death, the black night, is untellable because it is impenetrable shadow and despairing nonbeing, and because a wall that cannot be breached bars us from its mystery: unable to be spoken of, then, because there is absolutely nothing to say, rendering us mute, overwhelming reason, transfixing human discourse on the point of its Medusa stare. And the ineffable, in complete contrast, cannot be explained because there are infinite and interminable things to be said of it: such is the mystery of God, whose depths cannot be sounded, the inexhaustible mystery of love, both Eros and Caritas, the poetic mystery par excellence.

If the untellable, petrifying, all-poetic impulse induces *ability to produce new ideas* something similar to a hypnotic trance, then the ineffable, thanks to its properties of fecundity and inspiration, acts like a form of enchantment: it differs from the untellable as much as enchantment differs from bewitchment. Ineffability provokes bewilderment, which, like Socrates's quandary, is a fertile aporia. *Contradiction* "At a loss for words," writes Janáček for his part: where speech fails, music begins; when words are arrested, one has no choice but to sing.[59] Heine said it, too.[60] The ineffable unleashes a state of verve. *vigor/enthusiasm*

There will be things to be said (or sung) about the ineffable until the end of time. Who can possibly say, Now, everything is said? No. No one, ever, will be done with this Charm, which interminable words and innumerable musics will not exhaust, where there is so much to do, to contemplate, to say—so much to say, and in short, and again and again, of which there is everything to say. Among the promises made by ineffability is hope of a vast future that has been given to us. One delves without end into such transparent depths and into this heartening plenitude of meanings: if this plenitude is infinitely intelligible, it is also infinitely equivocal. The inexpressible–ineffable, being explicable into infinity, is the bearer of an ambiguous "message," in this, resembling Henri Bremond's "je-ne-sais-quoi." From a negative that is unsayable to a positive that is ineffable is a distance as vast as that between blind shadow and transparent night, or between silence that is mute, throttled, and silence that is tacit, for music takes root in the distant rumor of pianissimo, the border of silence. The meaning of the meaning is ineffable truth. If one considers life itself, then the meaning of the meaning is nothing more than a lethal absurdity—that is to say, death. The meaning of the meaning released by music is a mystery of the positive.

Reticence, generalized expression, and retrospective suggestion are, as we saw, paradoxically the most effective means of expression. Music signifies nothing at all, but a human being, in singing, stands at the meeting place of significations. Music is the ambiguous regime of the Espressivo that expresses nothing: in opposition to plain thought, sincere and serious thought conceived of necessity or expressing some present, particular idea, this or that, at this very moment, music knows nothing of the demands of nominalism. Thus polyphony itself is by definition equivocal or "plurivocal" since it conveys several heterogeneous and subterranean intentions simultaneously.

In language, words (which carry meaning) are naturally somewhat univocal: when equivocal—as homonym or synonym—they take part in a game played by virtuosos of the pun, a game played with sounds. The equivocal, however, is music's normal regime since it is a "language" that bears meaning only indirectly and suggests without signifying. The paradoxical mutuality of "being-in," the miracle of reciprocal inherence (inesse), fulfills itself at each step, in music. Consciousness, with its subconscious ulterior motives and its unconscious ulterior intentions, does not know the principle of contradiction: neither does music. The different themes in Pelléas et Mélisande are—at moments that flash by—almost

Music Example 1. Gabriel Fauré, Ballade in F-sharp minor for piano

immanent in each other, allowing for the expression of very subtle presentiments: music is not obliged to opt for this or that contradictory feeling.

With these contradictory sentiments, indifferent to any alternative, music creates a unique state of mind, a state of mind that is ambivalent and always indefinable. Music is, then, inexpressive not because expresses nothing but because it does not express this or that privileged landscape, this or that setting to the exclusion of all others; music is inexpressive in that it implies innumerable possibilities of interpretation, because it allows us to choose between them. These possibilities co-penetrate one another instead of precluding one another after the fashion of impenetrable bodies arrayed in

space, which exclude one another since each is fixed in its
own place. As an ineffably general language (if such is what
"language" should be), music is docile, lending itself to countless associations. Roussel attached the name "Evocations" to
three orchestral "images" inspired by India: but music, with
its double meanings, its readiness to oblige the most diverse
interpretations, will evoke just as easily anything it pleases us
to imagine. Sometimes music guides us, murmuring something, suggesting some unknown locale evoked in some pass-
able way. The lake at Wallenstadt, the evening in Grenada, a
mysterious name is whispered in our ear. Canopus, which rattles the poetic imagination, and yet, the name says to us, to
our soul: choose your chimera, imagine what you will, anything is possible.

This is, in sum, what Fauré wrote in 1906 with regard to
the andante movement of his second quartet, the only one of
his works in which a vague, external connotation—the sound
of the distant bells borne by the west wind, in a village in
Ariège—appears to sweep through the music, for a moment.
Now, this "thought" is so imprecise that it collapses into something better described as the *desire for nonexistent things*.[61] Fauré
made no specialty of the picturesque. Such is the indeterminate
poetic disposition that the extraordinary Ballade in F-sharp
minor infuses into our very being, into our ecstatic hearts: this
Ballade, which Joseph de Marliave sensed as something vernal
and sylvan, will for another seem charged with the ineffable
nostalgia of a past that has, once more, flown away.

The Ballade that is everywhere and nowhere, the distant
Ballade that is very near, may thus be an echo of youth in the
process of fleeing, or a familiar voice, the voice of irreversible
remembrance murmuring secret, untellable things into the ear
of our soul while evening descends. Yes: human beings recognize their own faces in this artwork composed of a charm
and of nonexistence, and in the incomprehensible disquiet
churned up in its wake.

Can we find it there, by chance—the thing we call music? The art of sounds—and this is said without metaphor—is the intimate interior, the heart of hearts of other arts. To acknowledge that music translates the soul of a human situation, and renders this soul perceptible to our soul's ear, one need not confer a vast transphysical reach upon music. In effect, physical sonority is already something mental, an immediately spiritual phenomenon: if the bells of Rimsky's invisible Kitezh, the metaphysical bells, cause audible harmonies to be heard, is this not because the music made by mere bronze is, already, supernatural?

t h r e e

THE CHARM AND THE ALIBI

THE POETIC OPERATION

The Charm's artwork—the "inexpressive Espressivo"—is not an act of Saying. Rather, it is an act of Doing, ποιεῖν (to do, make, or produce), and in this regard, music is similar to the poetic act.[1] "Make music!" Socrates is commanded by his dream, μουσικὴν ποίει καὶ ἐργάζου (compose and perform music): never stop working.[2] Making is of an entirely different order from Saying. Composing music, playing it, and singing it; or even hearing it in recreating it—are these not three modes of doing, three attitudes that are drastic, not gnostic, not of the hermeneutic order of knowledge? The composer, the performer as active re-creator, and the listener as fictive re-creator all participate together in a sort of magical transaction. The performer works with the first member of this trio, causing the work to come into being as vibrating air during a certain elapsed time; the listener, the tertiary re-creator, works in imagination with the first two, making half-sketched gestures.[3] To remake is to make, and a re-beginning is often the true beginning; the poet who makes and the performer who re-makes, the composer who invents and the listener who understands, production (primary "poetry") and re-production (secondary "poetry"), the original beginning and the continued beginning, initiative and repetition, may well follow the same path, in the same sense, from the same point of view, and form nothing more than a single act. The second time, though without chronological priority, is often as much an inaugural and inceptive instance as the first.

Henri Bremond has said that one must interpret the poetic experience by *remaking* it.[4] The performer is similar to a lover in re-making the primordial act as if he or she were the first to do it, as if there had never been anyone before who had done so; the basic elements of Euclidean geometry are being reinvented, each respectively and in isolation, each for someone, by himself, personally. But music (like a performed play) is an act in a more drastic sense, in a more dramatic sense: music is bound to an event fixed in historical time, which has a fixed date, on a page torn off the calendar; it has a privileged space in the hall, can be pinpointed in a daily schedule of events, and is localized in space. This event is the performance.

Poetry can be memorized and recited; poetry implies the rituals of declamation and exclamation. But what is such an "act" compared to that great adventure, the piano recital? A few quarter-hours of stratospheric tension and constant vigilance, presence of mind, sangfroid, concentrated courage, these, in themselves, are the militant reality of music for a pianist. Music does not exist in itself but only in the dangerous half-hour where we bring it into being *by playing it.* Eternal truth becomes a temporal operation and submits itself to happening, effectively, according to the limits of the timetable and the calendar. This is what is called "taking place." The duality of expression and inexpressiveness—that is, of infinite expression—resolves itself finally as the effectiveness of a single act.

Music has this in common with poetry, and love, and even with duty: music is not made to be spoken of, but for one to *do*; it is not made to be said, but to be "played." No. Music was not invented to be talked about.

And that, is it not, is also the definition of the Good. Good is made to be done, not to be said or known. And similarly Evil is a way of committing an act, more than it is something that can be known; Good and Evil, if not of the order of the dramatic, are at least of that of the drastic. Good is the affair of militants. Thus, poetry might be seen as a sort of beneficence. To do as one says, even to do without saying (thus the *Manual of Epictetus*): that could be the motto of all whose intentional, direct vocation is Doing, to do (as a transitive verb), to do purely and simply, and not to have done on one's behalf, to let be done. For what is a word if not a secondary action, an action with an exponent, or better yet (compare the rhetorical art of "persuasion") action taken upon an action? Saying is an atrophied version of Doing—miscarried Doing, a bit degenerate. Action in retreat, action simply sketched, the word is happy to be a pharisee, not acting, except indirectly.

Except (to be sure) in poetry, where it is Saying itself that is the Doing: the poet speaks, but these are not words meant to say something (like the words in the Civil Code) but, rather, are words to suggest or ensnare, the words engendering the Charm. Poetry is made to make the poem; and poetics, which is Doing with an exponent, to reflect upon poetry. In music, the same distinction characterizes the musician and the theorist. Nowadays, one talks too much to have anything to say, musically. So too philosophers, forgetting to do philosophy, speak of the next person's philosophy instead, and that next person, lacking any personal philosophy, speaks in his or her turn of the next person's philosophy, and so on into infinity, each one shaking a finger at the other, each referring to the others, thus fashioning a convenient alibi that releases philosophers from the responsibility of having their own opinions. But does the weapon's report—the echo from one *placitum* to another—transport us ultimately back to the first wise man who, not having a predecessor, was obligated to think for himself? Δόγματα (beliefs, opinions) form a channel of interference between us and πράγματα (things, acts), loosening our contact with the original: philosophy becomes doxography, even logology. Nowadays, the whole world talks, and disserts, and reasons.

And when in our turn we claim to speak of the untellable, let us speak of it, at least, by saying that it is not necessary to speak of it and by hoping that this constitutes the last time we will do so. The pretentious, intolerable mediocrity of most of the chatter on the subject of music is something profoundly depressing. This is not to say that actual musicology should be a priori suspect, and this by virtue of the fact that it is an exponent art: the most subtle musicologists are composers or practitioners; and doing and theorizing can be brought together, as they are by Rameau. Speculative lucidity and creative genius can be united. There is certainly no lack of musicians who unite them: Rimsky-Korsakov, Bartók, Dukas and Debussy, Schoenberg and Stravinsky. Yet lucid speculation has nothing in common with the sterile pedanticism of doctrinaire speculation.

More often, however, the composer has only one mode in which to reflect upon creation: to do it. His unprecedented neologisms will, themselves, become a precedent; hence Fauré, using antique modes without actually having conceived of doing so and recognizing only in retrospect that the hypolydian mode appears in the dance music of *Caligula*.[5] Hence Musorgsky and his fellow autodidacts, the Kuchkists, speaking a brilliant new language: and afterward the grammarians came along and pasted labels on their configurations. Hence Prokofiev, instinctively using atonal language when some unidentifiable impulse dictated the choice, looked at the reporter who questioned him about the "crisis of atonality" with as-

tonishment, because he never asked himself any such questions. His business is Doing, just as the nightingale's business
is singing and the bee's business is producing honey. A nightingale or a poet resembles a hero in this regard: a hero does
not read papers about heroism, and he is not heroic by virtue
of what he says but because of what he does. And nightingales
sing ornaments but do not give lectures about ornamentation.
And Fevroniya, the virgin of Kitezh, does not make reports to
some Institute but rises up, and the reindeer at her feet weep
with passion. The poetic operation's essential simplicity renders suspect all the messages, testimonials, and professions of
faith that artists make when, by chance, they prod themselves
into writing up the theory behind their creations. In general,
the creative imaginations are completely absorbed in a naive
state of being, taken up by the deep, blind toil of Doing.
Don't read what they profess, but listen to what they do. For
instance, don't read what Tolstoy the wise man is saying, read
what Tolstoy the novelist is doing.

The composer is like a singer who does not know how to
speak and can only sing, or a pianist who is asked to discuss
something and who sits at the piano without saying a word:
because—she knows it, and each listener understands it
straightaway—this is the way she will explain herself most
subtly, or best respond to our questioning. You are going to say
that this does not constitute an answer, and nonetheless this
mute answer is a *response*, and an unusually eloquent one, the
drastic, manual response of the musician. Liszt is remembered
for citing in the form of an epigraph the texts that inspired his
musical poems, a Petrarch sonnet, the sermon to the birds,
some verses by Lamartine, "Ce qu'on entend sur la montagne"
(Victor Hugo). But when the piano or the orchestra raises its
voice, something that is of an *entirely different order* assails us,
something diffluent and vague, where the voice of nature and
that of humanity are still indistinct, something that is no longer

chaos but is also not the world's planisphere: this "something" is the efficient, irrational order of music.

For the same reason, there are no dissertations on Fauré, as eloquent as they may be, that dare the depths that are plumbed in the act of listening to the second quartet, because the adagio movement of the second quartet is not a work that one can elaborate upon. One must give oneself over to the long, marvelous nocturne, the glowing sidereal serenity, to understand the viola's cantilena. An advance runner from "nonexistent things" and restless desire, ushering us into their presence, the cantilena says to us (maybe): "I have a great, unfulfilled departure within me" because that is the last phrase of *Horizon chimérique*, the chimerical horizon, and because those words might well be the musician's *ultima verba*. The unappeasable nostalgia will finally find peace, and the three last, quiescent pages of the Adagio—where the grand nocturnal phrase sinks gently into a pacific sea, into sleep—these pages defy all analysis just as they surpass any words.

This is no less true of the *Requiem*: because hearing the *Requiem* is an act, just as playing it is, and this unique but renewable event always adds something to the idea one has fashioned of the work, just as an actual performance—*performing* the piece *on the instrument*—will always entail something unforeseen in even the most detailed deciphering of the score. Anyone who has not heard an orchestra play the sanctus of the *Requiem*, heard the supernatural pianissimos being played, the harps' susurrations, the sovereign, stellar effusions of the choral passages, the narcotic cantilena of the strings, its modulatory feints, and all of this entire, muted, unknowable something, authentically "bergamasque," and not resembling anything else on earth: no one who has not *heard* this in a performance can recognize the Fauréian mystery or possibly know even the initial word of a charm that only Philistines would imagine can be described in advance. One needs to taste this fruit in all its sweetness to get an idea of it, because the taste, the hearing, is an experience that cannot be replaced, of a thing that is incomparable.

And similarly, no reading can substitute for the real love of a real woman, just as, in Proust, no description, however hallucinatory it may be, can convey an idea of Venice to those who have not gone there in reality and breathed its air personally. No human imagination can anticipate or represent the undefined elements in the Ballade in F-sharp without having tasted them. Those who have gathered the mystery of the six sharps under their fingers, however, and felt that mystery vibrating in black keys and white keys, will feel an *entirely other* resonance, something that no one can convey to someone else. There is not a single universe, but multiple universes, universes within universes between the Ballade that one subjects to a thematic analysis, and the Ballade one plays on ivory, on the piano; and the smell of Venice itself, as much as it is sui generis, is a wholly specific, crude quality next to the subtle intoxication and unrepresentable delirium, θεῖα μανία (divine enthusiasm), that the Ballade conveys to us. This Charm, which takes the form of a musical act, and the lyric intoxication that it engenders as response, are taken together Gabriel Fauré's "philosophy" in its entirely, just as Fevroniya's prayer in act 4 of *Kitezh*, and the ocean tsarina's lullaby in *Sadko*, are Nikolay Andreyevich's metaphysics in its entirety.

With this Charm (the musical act), there is nothing to "think" about, or—*and this amounts to the same*—there is food for thought, in some form, for all infinity; this charm engenders speculation inexhaustibly, is inexhaustible as the fertile ground for perplexity, and the same charm is born of love. Infinite speculation, as soon as it becomes exhilaration pure and simple, is analogous to the poetic state. Thus it is that the *Requiem* tells of trust, and the hope of another world, and that nostalgia is invisible and supernatural, and of many other things which Fauré himself doubtless never imagined. These things—Fauré tells of them in arpeggios, and does better still than "tell": his music plays them, and sings them, and suggests infinitely what no language can explain or express. Once the sacral arpeggios of the *Requiem* have dissolved into air—*in Paradisum deducant te angeli*—each listener has understood that there is no necessity for further commentary; everything has been said, and we exchange glances in silence, as Plotinus suggests, σιωπήσαντας δεῖ ἀπελθεῖν, "we must go away in silence."[6] Because once the soul has been upended by something immense and grave—after Boris's sublime singing at the end of act 2 of *Boris Godunov*, the supernatural silence that asserts itself at the end of the *Faust Symphony*, when the male choir comes onstage to sing the "Chorus mysticus"— nothing remains, except to be silent.

Thus Tolstoy describes the mystery of death: he who must understand it will understand it.[7] Music, as if it were a canticle sung by God, does not answer our questions directly. No, it is the pagan oracles that give answers when one goes to consult them, and they invariably say too much, these little, loquacious gods. And if they speak that way, it is doubtless because they know nothing. God, he himself, remains silent, preferring the answer in arpeggios or nightingales, the high cries of his swallows or the murmur of the prophetic leaves. Those who put a stethoscope to a nocturnal silence, to hear the imperceptible music of the spheres, the invisible harmonies, the bells of spiritual Kitezh, will hear a secret whispered by night: but the voices are distant and many, and the answers are confused. This is music's ambiguous way of answering. Music, like the divine nightingales, answers with the deed, by Doing. It is up to us to know how to grasp the message that has taken us prisoner.

FEVRONIYA, OR INNOCENCE

I say this with Aristotle: one becomes a kithara player *by* playing the instrument; it is only *by* plucking the harp's string that

one becomes a harpist. In poetic creation, as in an apprenticeship, the musician expresses himself during the creative operation itself, in the course of this operation. As for the music
thereby made, it will have signified something in retrospect.
Meaning takes shape in the present, is released in the future
perfect tense, and is never set in stone by the artist a priori.[8]
Only ideologues deliberate before doing. A priori, the musician does not intend to express a meaning but to sing: so, in
singing—that is to say, in the act of doing—he is expressing
himself, just as one becomes a smith by striking the iron, or
as Achilles demonstrates movement by lunging. Thus: first,
forge something, play something. Begin with "to make," sup-
posing the problem is already resolved, to resolve it in turn.
Begin with the end, and the rest will burgeon out for us without our even thinking of it, in the same way that youth ma-
tures; but if we overtly seek this "remainder," we will miss it
entirely.[9]

And music above all—even "pure" music—will find itself
expressing something quite adequately, so long as it did not
want to do so; and the musician will gain the sympathy of his
listener, above all, if—like Fauré—such recompense was un-
sought; just as serious, sincere remorse, truly desperate remorse, will perhaps be granted redemption, so long as remorse has not demanded redemption as the wage owed its
virtues. The overinformed conscience transforms despair into
theater of the Disperato. But grace has a surprise in mind,
and it sweeps us off our feet: the grace that is refused to those
who overact, whose repentance is interested or mercenary,
will fulfill us when we stop posing for the gallery or eyeing
our own merits, when the agent no longer usurps the position
of witness. Diotimus of Mantinea (Banquet, 210e), opposing
ἐφεξῆς (successively) and (sudden) ἐξαίφνης, says that if ini-
tiation is a gradual dialectics, contemplation is sudden: and,
in effect, one must have labored intensely to gain intuition.
But this is not to say that intuition shall be the obligatory

reward, the common result of all effort, because no one has a right to inspiration. The necessary condition is never sufficient; and as much as intuition is allied *in general* with inspiration (and that in a rather ambiguous way), intuition per se remains an essentially capricious and unpredictable benison. Whoever seeks God imperiously will never find him; but it may happen that someone who seeks innocently, and seeks without the least bit of self-satisfaction, will have already found him, by turning away from a mirror in which self-consciousness reflects his or her own image.

A certain state of innocence is no less vital in the artist:[10] the great innovators, like Chabrier, are those that create innovations without expressly having wished to do so, like Fauré, who do not try so avidly to make something new; as great innovators, Fauré and Prokofiev do not ask themselves so many questions. The small races, the aphid workers, they are the questioners. But first and foremost an artist makes music because he has something to say out loud and because he feels the need to say it, and afterward, what he has written will seem like a new entity, according to his inventiveness, his improvisatory spontaneity. True originality does not entail the express intention of creating *something new* and actually excludes the quest for novelty at all costs. "Wanting to say" is often the surest way not to convince anyone. Preaching puts us off and discourages our consent: anyone too eager to convince stops being convincing and, perversely, instills contradiction in his audience. "Better is the enemy of well." It is the dialectic of "too much" that watches over the neutralization of all forced expression, expression arranged with too heavy a hand. Tolstoy's *Anna Karenina* is more "instructive" than his didactic play *I svet vo t'me svetit* (*And the Light Shines in the Darkness*), in the way that any art work is more "instructive" than a sermon so easily seen through.

This is why propaganda is so weak, so ineffectual, hardly persuasive, why the propagandist needs to make a pretense of

spontaneity to entrap his audience. Alas! for feigned spontaneity itself becomes one stratagem in a strategy, and one can
no longer break out of the infernal circular trap of automatism. Propaganda that expressly acknowledges its purpose as a
form of publicity, instead of pretending naively to convey the
truth, becomes ipso facto inoperative.

The death of the hero, the sacrifice of the martyr, are not
propaganda. Specifically, heroes and saints are not part of
propaganda's regime: quite literally, they preach by example; it
is the person, the very presence of the hero, that teaches heroism.[11] Heroes are not eloquent in their discourse but by their
actions, by the mute example of their lives. That life is the sole
instance that exalts, that is radiant with aura, that communicates, that instills the urge to emulate; and only the effective
instance—whether poetic or heroic—is capable not just of
changing our minds but of changing our conduct. An orator
acts upon his listeners by conscious suggestion; that is, he
tries to influence, or flatter, or indoctrinate the listener; but
poets raise us up above ourselves by a sort of expansive contagion that is to suggestion as propaganda is to proposition.
There is a real chain reaction. As Valéry puts it, the poet engenders a state of inspiration in the reader.[12] Poetry induces a
sort of secondary poetry; and, just as freedom liberates those
who live within its compass, just as movement mobilizes the
inert bodies through which it travels, so poetry shouts at us
and renders us a bit poetic. Even the most prosaic individuals,
won over by this communicative enthusiasm, by divine delirium and contagious exhilaration, even they will burn with
inspiration in turn, and set themselves to sing.

Music, too, makes every listener into a poet, since music
has sole possession of a certain persuasive power, called the
Charm, and innocence is the condition for its existence. The
innocence of the performer in re-creating responds to the innocence of the composer in the midst of creation; thus, the
performer forgets the onlookers' stares, so absorbed is he or

she in bringing work into being, sustained ecstatically by the labor required to overcome obstacles. While this is happening, how could a performer possibly carve out the free time to allow self-consciousness to engender a split personality, or to strike attitudes for the gallery? The eloquent, mute lesson of Charm functions only by means of entirely spontaneous and nascent suggestion on the part of the agent. Because if the agent wants too much, then the one acted upon will no longer desire; if the agent begins to work too hard, then the one acted upon withholds his or her consent: and the Charm is broken. There are no recipes for charming, but perhaps there are recipes for being an enchanter, that is, for being a clown. All that is valuable and precarious (Angelus Silesius sensed this prior to Schelling)[13] is of the same order: one cannot *be* except in the condition of not *having*; one cannot *have* except in the condition of not *knowing*. "I do not know what I know," says Mélisande to Arkel, in act 5 of *Pelléas*: this is transparent innocence on its deathbed, astonished in the presence of consciousness and its anxieties.

Am I not saying the same thing? The most hallucinatory and revelatory expression is the one that has no desire to express or explain. Perhaps this is the sense in which one must understand the *exercitium occultum nescientis se numerare*, or, as Schopenhauer paraphrases Leibniz, *nescientis se philosophari*. The virgin Fevroniya (in *The Legend of the Invisible City of Kitezh*) was the sublime incarnation of this not-knowing, whose secret name is Innocence. Like Orpheus or Francis of Assisi, Fevroniya is at home in the company of swallows, or nightingales or tigers, being a little nightingale herself, *solovushka*; like the bard Sadko, she enchants wild animals and humanizes nature without knowing either how or why. "I don't know what I am going to sing. I only know that a song is ripening within me," writes the Russian poet Fet.[14] The Russian virgin in *Kitezh* is sister under the skin to those frank creatures of Debussy's imagination, Mélisande and the Girl with the Flaxen Hair. Fevroniya the pure, Fevroniya the wise, incarnates (with her sisters) Charm's innocent transactions; the Charm is graceful, without complacence, knowing no changes of heart or mind, no backtrackings upon reflection; it is the efferent force that surrounds gentle Fevroniya with her Flaxen Hair like an aura, and converts us every time.

At this point it will become evident that modern music, in certain respects, longed for a return to the spirit of childhood. The spirit of childhood suffuses Musorgsky's *Detskaya* (*The Nursery*) and Anatoly Lyadov's children's songs (along with Sergey Lyapunov's); one encounters it in Novák's *Mlady* as well as in Albeniz's *Yvonne en visite*. The new candor, the new aura that gives rise to child's play and mischief in Bizet, Debussy, Ravel, and Séverac, and Satie's babbling childishness, and Mompou's material ingenuity, and Koechlin's transparent sonatas, represents the spirit of childhood. With twentieth-century composers, no matter what names are cited, the "children's corner" gets bigger and bigger. Contemplating the seasons, the animals who crawl, fly, and bellow, the forest's enchantments, and the magic of metamorphosis, contemplating the "prodigious prodigies" that nature unfurls like a fantastic spectacle for eyes that are still chaste and naive, Ravel and Rimsky-Korsakov rediscovered the soul of a child in a state of wonder. Only innocence can attain the fresh, almost too-childish vision that was granted to Rimsky-Korsakov: innocence, because it is a form of purity, is the sole state capable of this kind of ecstatic objectivity.

Music, of all the arts, is in the end the one most alien to eroticism. Musorgsky's innocence, or Albeniz's or Ravel's, represent a marvelous lesson in reticence and chastity, set in opposition to the insufferable erotomania that is one reflection of contemporary cultural moroseness, of contemporary indifference in its most fatal form. Our terrible epoch, despite its pathological attachment to trash, has kept alive a great nostalgia for innocence and is not deaf to the voice that origi-

nates in a heart that is chaste and simple when that voice
makes itself heard.

THE SPATIAL MIRAGE

Up this point, I have spoken almost exclusively of the *rhetorical idols* that assimilate music to language. But the *optical idols*
are more tempting and more misleading still. The speaking
animal is also a visual animal and does not wholly grasp what
he projects into space. Spatial transposition is the metaphor
par excellence in this regard. The "metaphysics" of music, as
shown above, rests entirely upon a series of such metaphors.
We would need a second Bergson to root out the mirages of
spatialization that are scattered throughout musical aesthetics.
More than any other, the dubious, vague, controversial truth
of musical Becoming solicits metaphors: it is vision layered
upon hearing, and projects the diffluent, temporal order of
music into the dimension of space, onto spatial coordinates.
Images suggested by plastic arts, by painting or sculpture, are
the most common elements of fashionable aesthetic phraseol-
ogy. Often suggestive, sometimes suspect, the correspondence
between the arts invites us to consider music as a species of
architecture, magical architecture.[15] Music is nothing more
than "structures": plans, amounts, melodic lines, instrumental
colors.

   Yet one could ask oneself—language in toto having arisen
as means to translate visual experiences—whether there are
not, generally, other means to express the symphonic inexpressible or to tell the untellable sonata. The prepositions and
adverbs that we employ to describe relationships between melodic lines or sounds—"in," "above," "under"—are themselves spatial in origin. The analogy of colors and tonalities—
if one does not mistake it for a literal similarity—is it not
justified by the confluence of visual and sonorous impressions
in the seat of the consciousness that associates them, com-

pares them, and interprets one on the basis of the other, translates the same condition of the soul as different pianos, in different and heterogeneous registers?

In fact, three-quarters of all musical vocabulary, from Design to Form to Interval to Ornament, is borrowed from the realm of vision. Must we renounce it? But the aesthetics of metaphor wants more still: it wants the musical phenomenon to become a particular object, easy to locate; it aspires to answer the question *what* and the question *where* in unambiguous ways, the first by definitions and the second by localization. But exactly *where*, in the end, is music? Is it in the piano, or on the level of the vibrating string? Does it slumber within the score? Or maybe it sleeps in the grooves of the record? Is it to be found at the tip of the conductor's baton? In effect, the general characteristics attributed to "music" often exist only for the eye, by means of the conjuring trick of graphic analogy. The simple particularity of writing, which results from the symbolic projection of a musical act into two dimensions as a score, will suffice for us to characterize the melodic "arch"; and a melody that is outside all space, as a succession of sounds and pure duration, is subjected to the contagion of graphic signs inscribed horizontally on the staff. In the same way, the chord, a harmony composed of simultaneously perceived sounds, tends to be confused with the vertical aggregation of notes that form its schema; and the parts in polyphonic music seem to be "superimposed," placed in space on top of and underneath one another.

The artifices of staff paper end by dislodging acoustic realities. Bartók, in *Mikrokosmos*, writes two little pieces in which a funneling down of notes over a tonic pedal point translates as a graphic sign that evokes the opposition of the line and the point.[16] And who knows whether our sense that triplets "whirl" has not been suggested by our habitual association of the figure with its graphic trace on paper? Robert Siohan rightly denounces the "visualism" of certain procedures held dear by the Serialists, the "mirror games," the inverted forms, and so forth, since they are opaque to the ear.[17] One must also accuse the visualism of all those who talk about inversions, not to mention musical rhymes,[18] because to do so is to forget that music is made to be heard and not to be read, not at all, and to forget that symmetry, as a product of visual intuition, is not recognizable to the ear. Because, in effect, a trajectory in space can be traced by two senses, one applies the idea of a cycle or a round trip to music, as if musical movement were reversible. There may be a memory of something repeated, but there are no symmetries, nor is there a "center" of an irreversible Becoming, oriented in one direction, where even the recapitulation *takes over*, and where the *seconda volta*— even if indistinguishable from the first—differs from it imperceptibly by the mere fact of its secondary position, that is, by the simple chronological priority of the first time. The arrival of the future, without excluding memory, prevents the circle from ever being closed.

Musical experience can also be contaminated by kinesthesic impressions: Nikolay Cherbachov's *Rouet* appears to owe its title to the oscillating motion of the left hand above the right hand and the undulation that results, on the keys, by the crossover. Associations that are established though sounds in combination with the movements of the hands on an instrument,[19] between music and its choreographic parsing out, between the attenuation of sound by distance and the experience of spatial displacement: all these compete to create an auditory space around us, a hybrid milieu in which music rises and falls, becomes distant (in getting softer), and possesses a high and a low, just like space itself; this choreography serves to dot the "i" in the spatial metaphor. And such nativism is not necessarily wrong: there is a concrete space that all sounds aspire to construct. But the idea of the voluminous and (as we saw) of musical "depth" does not in itself have meaning in relation to time; it is time that makes the Charm evasive and diffuse, which takes the "ipseity" of music and grants it absei presence that is infinitely fugitive and disappointing.

In the entirely different order of musical temporality, th same will in turn always appear other than itself. Music is not calligraphy projected into space, but a lived experience analogous to life. One need only remember that music is addressed to the organ called *ear*.

TEMPORALITY AND THE NOCTURNE

There is no reason, perhaps, to further belabor the point that all philosophies of music are a perilous wager involving continuous acrobatic feats. I have refused to grant music the power of discursive development, but not the power to trace an experience of lived time. Fauré and Séverac embark on this "gentlest path"[20] that so many others follow. Such wandering is always a bit dream-like and nocturnal: this is Becoming. Fluid and without an itinerary: such is music. The dimension it assumes is made of all that is least palpable and most evanescent, and this dimension, Becoming, is a state that Aristotle has already declared to be quasi-nonexistent, since one does not conceive of it except in twilight thought, as if through the mist of dreaming. Becoming does not permit the object to be divided into sectors, according to its corporeal limits; it is much more the dimension according to which the object undoes itself without end, forms, deforms, transforms, and then re-forms itself. A succession of states of the body, that is, change itself, dissolves the limits fossilized by our mental habit of splitting and dividing.

Variation and Metamorphosis correspond to this regime of continuous mutation, music's regime par excellence. The theme—the insignificant object of the variation—negates itself amid the reincarnations and metamorphoses; the "grand variation" is not a process of modeling a plastic object but much more that of modifying little by little, modification that is modulating, modification without a mode, without even a substance of which the modality would be a "mode," without a being of which "ways of being" would be the ways. Maybe the quality of temporal fluidity explains Fauré's predilection for the supple, ravishing continuity of the Barcarolle, as in *Le Ruisseau, Au bord de l'eau, Eau vivante.* The Heracletan changeability of flowing water was for Bergson the sensory image of lived time. In this regard, Fauréian continuity is closer to Bergson than Debussyian discontinuity, and the thirteen *Barcarolles* are more "Bergsonian" than *La Mer*; and the barcarolle of the living waters more Bergsonian than the still water of Impressionism.

Water in motion drowns form, and night blurs its contours. Music is, then, naturally nocturnal; even mid-day music is nocturnal, being still twilight on one side, as in Debussy's three symphonic *Nocturnes*. Fauré's forest canopy is twilit, dream-like, and so is Séverac's azure and even Rimsky-Korsakov at his most solar. Satie, a nine o'clock in the morning composer, wrote five *Nocturnes* for piano. With musicians, light does not etch with precision or localize in space, but conceals. With Fauré, it is not just thirteen "Nocturnes" that are nocturnal: the Barcarolles are, too, and even the Valses-Caprices, the Ballade in F-sharp, the andante of the second quartet, the first piano prelude. In *Caligula*, when the "Hours of the Night" are abandoned in favor of the martial rhythms of the "Hours of Day," chords enter into a state of fusion: as stripped arpeggios, made liquid, unfurled, they accompany the flow of the dreaming Dumka. With its motile shadows and confused murmurs, Scriabin's op. 61, *Poème nocturne*, is the poem sung by Dionysian dissolution. So many Berceuses, Serenades, Nocturnes, Clairs de lune: they all bear witness to music's enduring preference for that privileged moment when form and images dim into the indistinct, moving toward chaos, and for midnight, which submerges all multicolored patterns into its great shadow. The first element is the shipwreck that is sleep; the second is nocturnal diffluence per se; the first is hypnotic, and the second of the order of dreams.

It is the gray landscape of evening that melts the spatial divisions of high noon; but it is the nocturnal blackening of the world that sinks and submerges the static coexistence of singular things, and forces a blinded consciousness to proceed in a new way, gropingly. For an observer who is perched in the observatory, protected by the heights he commands, everything can be seen together; he grants himself global vision, immediate vision, cavalier toward the existences that unfold below, where dramas are being rolled out like a tapestry. This is the optics of spectatorship, the contemplative viewpoint, won by surveillance. The human being who sees is *looking* in order not to *be*.

The musical universe, however, does not lie there exposed to the mind or proposed to the mind: music, no matter how objectivist its aspirations, inhabits our intimate center; we live music, as we "live" time, as a fertile experience, with the ontic participation of our entire being. Night helps to transform a "speculative" quandary into a drama that we live. Even when a composer (such as Liszt or Musorgsky)[21] chooses some painter's tableau or some sculptor's statue as a pretext for his musings, he transposes optic actuality into the nocturnal dimension of Becoming: the listener will experience events one after another, where elements are given to the spectator to see at the same time, that is, in a timeless Now. When night deprives consciousness of its synoptic, panoramic view of the world, that consciousness will be plunged into the immanence of darkness and will test things and objects as it goes along, little by little, as a succession of events. Even Liszt, at the summit of the high peak where he was summoned by Victor Hugo, does not see the universe like a Mercator projection spread out at his feet: he cannot dominate what he *hears* on the mountain, but by means of music, he is engaged, temporally: simultaneous places, which an effect of altitude distributes and deploys as if on an atlas, become musical *moments* sensed one by one. Visual coexistence escapes into musical diffluence. A human being is suspended over the world or contemplates the world as if it were a fresco: but now, that same person is immerged and allows a form of Becoming to take place, and it carries him away. The fresco, which was of the spatial order of coexistence, begins to flicker and unroll, as if it were a film.

This is why the Charm is proper to music. If Beauty consists in nontemporal plenitude, in the fulfillment and parsing out of form, in static perfection or morphological excellence, then the Charm has something nostalgic and precarious about it, some unknowable something having to do with insufficiency and incompleteness, which heightens itself through the effect of time. The Charm does not provide us with the solution to a problem but is much more a state of infinite aporia that produces a fruitful perplexity; and in this, is more ineffable than untellable. The Charm is always coming into being: because succession does not grant us a present moment except by concealing an anterior moment, and this alternation creates all that is melancholy in temporality.

Thus music, at an extreme, develops an inexpressible perfume, the scent of all the memories that disturb and age a soul slowly suffused by knowledge of the past-ness of its own past. "Gilded days of my youth, what distance now harbors you?" asks Vladimir Lensky, only an instant before the fatal duel that will pit him against Onegin.[22] The poet Aleksey Tolstoy in turn has known the sadness of Olympio, and he asks the specter of reminiscence, "Do you recall, Marie, the time that is lost?" The event, fugitive and irreversible, the evanescent quality, absence, an occurrence long gone by that will never be once more—these are musical melancholy's privileged objects. Is music not a form of enchanted temporality? Idealized nostalgia, nostalgia reassured and purged of all specific anxiety? For if it is entirely temporal, music is at the same time a protest against the irreversible and (thanks to reminiscence) a victory exacted from the irreversible, a means of resuscitating the same in the form of the other.

In music, we would say, repetition is not needless repetition. Thematic reminiscence seems already anterior to the ear, an evasive and allusive evocation that conceals even as it conjures up. Musical reminiscence is the art of keeping, or of remembering. *Nezabudka*, "Forget-me-not." Arensky's meditation (op. 36, no. 10) on a pressed flower expresses fidelity to the past, in its own language, the cult of distant things, things long gone and, depite that, precious beyond counting, the poet's attempt to arrest the flight of the hours or the days. When the massive initial phrase of Fauré's sixth *Nocturne* emerges right before the end of the piece, out of the A major shaft suspended like vapor along the entire range of the piano once, *after* the sustained pedal point, the pedal is taken off little by little, then this great nocturnal phrase meets our recognition of it like a distant and faithful friend. And in truth, that fraternal past had never abandoned us. The theme itself: is it not—within the flow of the melody's Becoming—a sort of affective reminiscence, a hint of memories that cannot be described? Such are the disquieting *Vzpomínání* with which Josef Suk closes off his *O matince* (*About Mother*). When peace returns to us, at last, then it happens sometimes that we rediscover an echo of childhood, a memory of the vernal that will never again exist, a familiar voice and its singing: what a mother sang when she was herself a small child, what mothers sing in the night to children lying sick in bed, the maternal heartbeat itself. Suk's *O matince* and Fauré's sixth nocturne are taken together, each in its own way a digest of lived time; both end dreamily, as lives sometimes do, with an escape from tempests and trials, in the meditative serenity of a long evening.

DIVINE INCONSISTENCY.
THE INVISIBLE CITY OF KITEZH

Under such circumstances, one easily understands the state of exaggeration that music creates in its listeners. Those four men dressed in black, who are not narrating anything, who grow joyous or sad over nothing while gesticulating in emptiness: that is a string quartet. What does Tolstoy find to reproach in this quartet of the vanities? He reproaches it for engendering a kind of empty exaltation in us, a source of feelings that have no object, groundless melancholy or unmotivated enthusiasm. Mikhaíl Lermontov, in *A Hero of Our Time*, speaks of irrational joy and illusory sadness, born of music. Better still: music creates a state of deceptive lucidity, a state of false gnosticism; in the work per se, music is the bearer of specious transparency that is no more than impenetrable opacity, pseudo-evidence that is no more than pure confusion; after music blurs my brain, I believe that I have understood what I have not understood; in the instant that I lose my head to the Carian muse, I seem to feel what I have not felt and to be capable where I am incapable. Music smuggles in possibilities that are as wholly new as they are imaginary, transporting me into another realm entirely. What Tolstoy found scandalous was the shocking, improper disproportion between the depth of my emotion and mere melodious noise. He had no wish to deliver himself to black causality, to the fraudulent etiology that twists our heads the wrong way around. Years after *The Kreutzer Sonata*, his condemnation of music was affirmed in *And the Light Shines in the Darkness* and his book *What Is Art?* provided the theoretical framework: music, which causes us to forget everything, serves only to put off a dilemma; music obscures, being a typical instance of apparent illumination, false light in the darkness.

In fact, he is being a bit unjust about the raptures that have staggered us: the person listening to the ineffable has hardly an idea how he might rise up to the heights of his experience. Confronted with Chopin's *Andante spianato*, or the adagio of Fauré's second quartet, one feels as one does on the day when the first winds of spring blow, the day of the very first softness, of the first lilac scent: emerging from a narrow place, from winter's moroseness, anyone who has been upended by this new warmth, exhilarated by the sun and its promise of renewal, will ask himself what he will do, what he will say to be worthy of such a spectacular celebration. Will he, in turn, put on his best party clothes? Poeticized by universal poetry, will he in his turn write a poem? Maybe he will fall in love, yielding to the outburst, to the sweet matinee with its masses of flowers, by succumbing to the first feminine smile he encounters. Because loving is also a way to make poetry. And someone older, who seeks to join the low, vernal hum, discovers something more clear and chaste than he himself can be, and as recompense for all these unearned gifts, wishes for the power to manifest an untellable gratitude. We express our admiration and our recognition is such maladroit forms, but in clumsiness one sees something like humility, which is felt by individuals who stand before the incomprehensibility of a freely given gift. So forgive those who listen to the *Andante spianato* and do not know how to express their thanks, or to become equal to their experience; forgive them if they celebrate something incommensurable with all celebration in the wrong way: since one does not approach the ineffable except in stammering. As St. John of the Cross put it: "Balbuciendo."

In truth, it is the inconsistency of musical reality (so discouraging) that explains all the exaggerations and the chatter: one does not know what to get hold of or which object to examine; and everyone bypasses this question.[23] First the listener, who pretends to listen, but in fact, listen to what? To what does one pay attention? The listener believes that he understands something where, in reality, there is nothing to understand. The object of this immaterial; inapplicable attention, the musical object precisely speaking, is itself impalpable and unattainable, nonexistent. Never believe the silly people whose brows are furrowed with meditation as they pretend to be "following" theme A and theme B, with their faces thus ravaged by a string quartet. Follow: this is once again a dialectical-rhetorical analogy summoned by illusions of discursive development and the musical itinerary. The master leads and the listener "follows." It all seems too clear and simple: one recognizes a theme, gathers a harmony in passing, notes a phrase in the oboe—take all this together and one has "followed." There is something truly strange about the boundless seriousness with which listeners apply themselves to harmonic mumbling that is void of signification; there is something comical—if one recalls that humans are frivolous and their worries futile—in the religious silence that they maintain at concerts, in their maniac fear of being distracted. Distracted from what, then? The serious gentleman, listening with his eyes closed, is in fact thinking about the office.

But that is not his fault, if it is truly the case that no one thinks in any sincere way about music. One no more thinks about music itself—ipsa—or about music in actuality than one *thinks of time.* Anyone who believes he is thinking of time, in the sense that "time" is the direct complement or the object of a transitive thought, is thinking of events that take place in time or objects that endure in time, is thinking not of pure Becoming but of contents that are "coming into being." And in the same way, someone who imagines he is thinking of death (a case about which there is, by definition, nothing thinkable) is daydreaming but not thinking. This is why the "meditation upon death" is an entirely empty as mediation, as empty as the cenotaph before which the mourner collects his or her thoughts; this is why reflections upon death, not having found their handholds, so often resemble a state of somnolence.

Is this not the case with all ruminations about God or the night sky? Attention paid to music will never seize the intangible, unattainable center of musical reality, but swerves more or less toward the circumstantial sidelights of this reality: the thoughts of a listener plunged into process of listening, busy feigning the attitude of the acolyte in the sanctuary, are empty contemplation. One doesn't think about "music," but, on the other hand, one can think according to music, or in music, or musically, with "music" being made into the adverb that refers to a way of thinking. Those who believe they are thinking about music are thinking about something else, but more often still, are thinking about nothing—since all such pretexts are useful in avoiding hearing. Between the listeners who think of something else and the listeners who are simply asleep, all degrees of somnolence and daydreaming have been spanned.

Igor Stravinsky has made fun in spirit of such futile manifestations of melomania.[24] Most people demand from music nothing more than light intoxication, which they need as background accompaniment for their free associations, a rhyme to support their musings, a rocking cradle for their ruminations. Music no longer serves their purpose, for instance, when enveloping a drama in the lyric atmosphere of opera. For them, it has become home-furnishing music, in Satie's ironic sense, melodious rumbling heard under the meal and the chitchat: not "accompanied declamation," or (speaking with Albéric Magnard) "tragedy in music,"[25] but musical background for busy people. So the listener says: let's think about something else. And the musicologist decides in turn: let's talk about something else. For instance, the composer's biography, or his erotic affairs, or his historical significance. Conference-goers babble pleasantly, or roar, or wail. And writers, not knowing what to grasp hold of, come up with the idea of adoring musicians for reasons that have nothing to do with music: one will be interested in Debussy or Satie, for instance, because of the seductive literary or artistic implications in their works and will neglect Fauré because he says far less to the imagination of a painter or a novelist.

The most pedantic will speak of grammar, or craft, and are the most cunning of all, because they appear to aim at specifically musical realities, which can be pinned down in certain locutions, and since, for them, the affectation that is technical analysis is simply a means of not sympathizing, not being touched by the Charm, of sundering the covenant made with innocence and naïveté, on which all enchantment depends. Having heard the violinist-magician, the stalwart spirit that analyses the bowing, goes through the left hand and the forearm with a fine-tooth comb, discusses sonority and pizzicato, means to prove by all this that he has not been duped and does not consent to bewitchment. Because stalwart spirits know no weakness. Everyone knows the type, the cool cerebral people who affect interest in the way the piece is "put together" after the concert. Technical analysis is a means of refusing to abandon oneself spontaneously to grace, which is the request the musical Charm is making. The phobia about consent, the fear of appearing bewitched, the coquetry of refusal, the resolve not to "submit," are the social and sociological forms assumed by alienation, just as the spirit of contradiction is a form of mimicry. Maniac antihedonism is the mark of the technician and is akin in its frivolity to a love for Viennese waltzes.

A lapidary conclusion: almost no one speaks about music, musicians even less than others. And similarly: no one truly speaks of God, above all, not theologians. What is necessary is music itself, in itself, αὐτὴ καθ᾽ αὐτήν as Plato put it, and not music in relation to something else, or circumscribed. Alas, music in itself is an unknowable something, as unable to be grasped as the mystery of artistic creation—a mystery that can only ever be grasped "before or after." Before is the psychology, the character of the creator, anthropology. After is the description of the entity that came into being. How to capture the divine instant between the two, the thing that would be so critical to know and that is most obstinately hidden from us? Music's irritating, confusing secret is evasive and seems to taunt us.

Musical reality is always somewhere else, like Fauré's landscapes, evoked by means of evasive expressions with double meanings; this spiritual geography, where the Alibi perpetually blurs and clouds over the pinpointing of place, this geography makes all localization fugitive, fleeting: would we not say that music, as a temporal phenomenon, in general refuses spatialization?

One of Andersen's fairy tales, *The Bell*, is admirable in the ways that it makes this clear. A bell sounds mysteriously in a forest, and no one knows the location of the church or bell tower from which this marvelous sound issues. In reality, it is the great church of nature, of poetry, the omnipresent and omniabsent church, that sounds the Alleluia of the invisible sacred bell. The country of dreams, no one's country, the homeland of nonexistent things, the mystic Jerusalem of Fauré's *Requiem*, the invisible city, the otherworldly city of Kitezh, all these designate the doubtful homeland of a Charm that is not here, and not there, but everywhere and nowhere. "Your soul is a chosen land." And just as the soul challenges all cerebral localization, and God terrestrial localization, so celestial Kitezh, Kitezh that is absent and omnipresent, far and near, which is pure music itself, exists on no map. The city of Utopia, like the Neoplatonists' φίλη πατρίς (beloved homeland) and the troubadour's faraway country, escapes all topographies.

With Fauré, Hellenism affirms an indifference to the ethnographical or geographical picturesque, rather than invalidating it. Like Satie—the author of *Socrate*—Fauré never visited Greece. Hellenism, for them, represents more than the school for understatement and sobriety; beyond this, it signifies abstract pureness, the bareness of the *gymnopédie*, the atemporal, the absence of all distinguishing marks as of all local color. In the *Hymne à Apollon* reconstructed by Reinach, Fauré glorifies the waters of Castalia, Κασταλίδος εὔυδρου νάματα (the streams of well-watered Castalia).[26] "Castalia, cold, pure fountain, virginal and transparent water," as Michelet says.[27] Castalia the source of colorless water, chaste water that has no taste, like the water of Ilissos; Phaedrus and Socrates wander along its banks, καθαρὰ καὶ διαφανῆ τὰ ὑδάτια (waters pure and clear).[28] When Stravinsky renounces the Asiatic mode (*Le Sacre du Printemps*), or the Russian (*Petrushka*), or folklore (*Les Noces*), he does so to fall in step behind Apollo as leader of the Muses. What composers demand from Ancient Greece is neither dance rhythms nor popular songs, but a geographical dissolution compounded equally of ubiquity and Utopia. And yet music splashed with the colors of the picturesque, the Iberian mode, the Oriental mode, the Exotic mode, are, once more, a means of fleeing from that which *is*. The "dancer" in Fauré's *Mirages*, in this sense, is not more unreal that Borodin's Polovtsian maidens, and Mélisande, born "far from here," is no more distant than Fevroniya.

THE BERGAMASQUE CHARM.
MELODY AND HARMONY

A charm—like a smile or a look—is *cosa mentale*. What causes it? What does it consist of? Does it consist of anything to begin with? What is its place, its physical seat? Such things are not exclusively of the subject or of its object; rather, they pass from one to the other like an astrological influence. One can make the more general point that nothing is musical per se, neither a ninth, nor a dominant chord, nor a plagal cadence, not a modal scale—but anything can become musical, given the correct circumstances. Everything depends on the moment, the context, the occasion, and a thousand conditions that can transform an acoustic novelty into spiritual insincerity or pedantry, or make a brilliant discovery out of a banal little chord. Thus, there is no wholly unambiguous criteria, no decisive mark that enables us to differentiate between the Charm and its counterfeit, the authentic from the simulacrum. A simple F major arpeggio serves as the initial theme in Dvořák's Symphony op. 76; yet that arpeggio harbors so many thoughts, moving and profound thoughts: it is inspired. With Emmanuel Chabrier, it is easy to point out the compositional inventions that make the musical language in *Le roi malgré lui* or *Sommation irrespectueuse* (to a text by Victor Hugo) so savory and unusual: a undiscovered sequence, an aggregation of sounds, an unexpected modulation. But this would simply tally up grammatical turns, orthographical idiosyncrasies, and such things are a matter of indifference without the verve that brings them to the fore at a particular moment and that withholds their delights at others.

Even the famous musical innovations whose invention is rightly attributed to Debussy's creative genius, even these would be mere curiosities and, in the long run, rhetorical formulae, commonplaces, tiresome clichés, and stereotypes, were it not for a celestial, unknowable something that renders them eloquent and convincing from the outset. For a whole-tone scale per se is nothing, clearly nothing, and a series of parallel seventh chords is also nothing: at best a cliché, something for imitators to get hold of, a mechanical process suitable for industry and assembly-line production. Debussy's revolutionary innovations seem unforeseeable before the fact (or to anyone who seeks to anticipate them), surprising in the moment, and organically necessary after the fact or upon retrospective reflection. And it goes without saying that the same would have to be said of the exquisite innovations of a Ravel, so easily imitated, so quickly standardized by his epigones: major seventh chord, eleventh chord.

Music Example 2. Fauré, *Le plus doux chemin* (mm. 10–12 and 28–33)

With Gabriel Fauré, the opposite is true: novelty is more diffuse and does not owe anything (except vaguely) to details that can be isolated. Fauré in this sense is to Debussy as Chaikovsky was to Musorgsky: the language in general is new, insidiously so. But Fauré is nonetheless "French" as Chaikovsky is "Russian," through an unknowable atmospheric something that gives his music its local climate and that is never due to this or that identifiable Gallicism. This miracle assumes form as a subtle harmonic atmosphere, as a music that, apparently, makes use of the most ordinary locutions and never seeks elaborate, quintessential sonorities.

Of course, it is easy to note the decorative, distinctive

marks that are supposedly characteristic of Fauré's language. But someone who enumerates the marks has still said nothing. Someone who knows all the marks knows nothing if he or she does not know the exact *manner* and occasion. It is Fauré's *manner* that would need to be defined, and the grammarian has not gotten any farther than he or she was at the outset. The problem of the inexpressible remains unsolved, eternally problematic; it imposes a regression to the infinite. What is important in Fauré's *Ballade* in F-sharp is not the three motifs that can be analyzed and taken apart—the nocturnal motif of the opening section, the allegretto motif, and a motif sketched two times as a slow improvisation, then developed sometimes as an oscillating barcarolle rhythm, sometimes as a cheerful scherzo, sometimes as a trill. No, the important thing is the winged enigma, the "arcanum maximum," the almost-nothing without which the themes would be no more than what they are. And no more can one pin down a Charm sui generis, χάρις ἐπιθέουσα (grace diffused), the indefinable and irreducible strange flavor that impregnates the Andantino entitled *Le plus doux chemin.*

Is this Charm a consequence of sonority? Of nostalgic quietude, in the form of a plagal cadence? Or perhaps it derives from the Aeolian flavor of the leading note in the context of an equivocal F major? None of these. And still: raise the leading tone by a half-step; replace the fourth degree of the scale with a dominant, change the melancholy G-flat of the last measures into a G-natural, change just one note of the *Offertoire* or the end of the piano prelude in D minor, and everything will become banal and fall flat. Does this mean that the fourth degree of the scale or the interval of a seventh is the actual locus of the Charm? Something that could be dispelled with the slightest breath—is it created by an accidental, a flat sign? One could say rather that in changing a single note, one has substituted one totality for another: the diatonic realm, with its raised leading tone, replaces the modal. Henri Bergson and Henri Bremond have already noted that by displacing a single syllable within the verse, by changing the least of vowels, one vandalizes the entire poem.[29] The damage is disproportionate to the material alteration; the unknowable something has become unrecognizable.

A brilliant musician can in fact be an innovator without strictly speaking being an inventor. In such cases, those who expect "great discoveries" will be disappointed. Let there be no doubt: the rapacious need for novelty, so characteristic of the escalating modernist auction, entails the idea that a musical act is a *thing*, in which case, music is no more than technique, technique alone. And just as technique is the consequence of an indefinite process of perfection—with each automobile or kitchen appliance show ushering in what is new and improved in comparison to last year's—so perpetual progress shall be the law of music.[30] Farther, faster, more powerful! In this arms race, each new music, shattering its predecessor's records, offers itself as the last thing in modernity; and each musician, forcing predecessors into the category of the unfashionable and outmoded, claims the patent on the invention. In an era where pastiches of "scientific investigation" have become quasi-universal, musicians owe it to themselves to become "researchers" just like everyone else. But what are they looking for, in the end? A previously unknown chord? A new musico-atomic particle? It is a safe bet that a decline in inspiration translates into this thirst for innovation. Scriabin was a genuine "researcher" because he was inspired as well. And vice versa, those with nothing to say attached exaggerated important to novelties of vocabulary.

The essence of music in fact never consists in this or that. One could, however, ask more specifically whether this essence resides in melody, or harmony. Presented as a choice between alternatives, the question is unanswerable, and the debate between the adherents of melody and those of har-

mony could last until the end of time. Melody in itself is
nothing; harmony in and of itself is nothing. And harmoniza-
tion is scarcely more. An unharmonized melody is indifferent,
a harmony with no melody is dead, since a chord, even a
clever one, is a simple curiosity once it is no longer an element within a rhythmic succession: it lacks soul, being a rare
object, a precious gem, nothing more. A chord that is not
integrated within the before and after of a rhythmicized,
directed Becoming, a chord not endowed with signifying
force—this chord, like a neologism or a sampling of grammar, is arrested at the stage of nontemporal materiality.

Sometimes one hears it said that if harmony is music's
body, then melody is its "soul": but no one, ever, has seen a
soul without a body; nor strictly speaking a body without a
soul, since at the moment the body is deprived of life, it starts
losing its organic form to decomposition and becomes a ca-
daver. Music in turn is indissolubly "psychosomatic"—a lost,
wandering melody remains indeterminate and unanchored
until the moment when harmony gives it a meaning, just as
the bass pitches give singing its signifying intention, and
sometimes unexpected powers. Neither the vertical (which is
dead) nor the horizontal (which is completely bare and lin-
ear) will contain the essence of a musical event. Monody, for
its part, is not a complete organism, except on occasion, as a
tour de force, with the proviso that it should create its own
accompaniment (as Georges Migot says), which is only possible by virtue of the listener's auditory memory, and the play
of repetitions and ornaments, which create harmonic ether to
surround the single line.[31] This is, notably, the case in Migot's
monodies and in Debussy's flute solo *Syrinx*. Bartók and Prokofiev love the *unisono*;[32] but in Musorgsky, the single line
doubled at the octave reclaims its voluminous sonority.

Melody and Harmony refer to each other constantly: a
paradoxical inversion of received ideas enables Françoise Ger-

vais to style Fauré as the harmonist and Debussy as the melo-
dist,[33] meaning that Fauré's melodies lend their modal flavor
to the harmonic language while Debussy's aggregate chords
are at the disposal of melody, which they illuminate with their
many iridescent hues. Would the linearity of Fauré's songs be
as persuasive without the subtle finery that augments it? Music, we must finally admit, which cannot be pinpointed as
here or there, cannot be defined as this or that.

And concerning the analogy of music and poetry, I would
say: the charm of the Charm, like the meaning of meaning, is
present in the totality of the poem, yet it is never present in
this word or that, this verse or that. No matter how carefully
you dissect the cerebral membranes, you will not find
thought, nor will the microscope's eye light upon life *itself* in
scrutinizing the cell's nucleus and the chromosomes in the
nucleus and the genes within chromosomes, no more than
you can read the enigma of death in the last breath of the
dying, or the enigma of God in the blinking of stars, even if
you narrow your eyes and concentrate as hard as you can.
Meditating upon the star-filled sky, like meditating upon
death, is as unfathomable as it is empty. Similarly, anyone
who seeks music *somewhere* will never find it: our curiosity
will end up disappointed if we aspire to some revelation of
who-knows-what anatomy of musical discourse. But if we
agree, in the end, that we are dealing with a mystery and not
some material secret, with a Charm and not a thing; if we
understand that this Charm is wholly dependent on human
intention, on the moment in time, the spontaneous lurch of
our hearts; if we realize that such a Charm is fragile and not
always obvious to our minds and is allied to so many imponderable factors; that it depends first and on foremost on our
own honesty; then and only then will we know how to consent to this, the Charm created by music, which is the only,
true state of Grace.

ALLEGRETTO BERGAMASQUE. PIANISSIMO
SONORE, FORTE CON SORDINA

To speak of Kitezh—the city that cannot be spoken of—one would need either to restrict oneself to the negative propositions of apophatic theology, or to take two contradictory affirmations—which crash like cymbals, one against the other—and apply them simultaneously to the Charm, without ever exhausting its infinite essence. The latter amounts to the same thing as the former. More still: to define this intangible meeting of opposites, to put a puzzling mystery into words, innumerable paired predicates—where each is contradicted by the other—would not suffice. Even Verlaine, or Watteau, or Vermeer, is inadequate to conveying an idea of the particular evasive Charm of Fauré's music, the Fauréian Spell, which one is tempted to call "bergamasque"—like the penumbra, it involves a particular mélange of light and mystery.

A certain characteristic ambiguity, the element of contrast that signals the ineffable message, can be sensed in many great composers. Ravel was as simple as he was refined, and the fundamental ingenuousness of his heart stands in contrast to the stratospherically subtle complexities of his art. With Albeniz, all those sumptuous, rich harmonies cannot manage to conceal a quasipopular simplicity of inspiration. Despite his polyphonic craft, Bartók never loses the red thread of the melody. In spite of all the sarcasm, and the incredible violence, Prokofiev remains a virginal soul, so long as he stays within his white kingdom, C major. At once ingenuous and wise, like schooled ignorance; naive and cunning, like childhood; tender but impassive, like a heart kept secret; present and absent, like God; and familiar yet distant, like Death; patent yet latent, like the soul; at once translucent and mysterious, clear and deep, like a summer night, or like the lake in Rimsky-Korsakov's *Nuit de mai*, where chimeras are set dancing in the moonlight, like all these, Fauré's bergamasque

Charm envelops the peaceful cantilena in the *Agnus dei* of the *Requiem,* and in the *Plus doux chemin.*

The enharmonic equivocations,[34] the modality that avoids disjunction between major and minor, are symptoms of a deeper ambiguity. These antinomies are inherent in the Charm atmospherics, and from the performer they demand certain qualities that are similarly incompatible. For instance: amid all the puzzling contradictions of a system of metronome markings that is essentially evasive and ambiguous, how is one to discover the "moderate velocity," the *tranquil speed* whose name is allegretto, the Fauréian tempo par excellence? This is the speed at which the seventh variation of the *Theme and Variations* should be played, a variation that is both fussy and nonchalant and that must be played throughout with no pedal. Fauré's second *Impromptu* also demands that the pianist stay within the beat, without hurrying, resisting the temptations held out by the cataracts of chords and avalanches of precious stones and diamond rains. For acceleration is a suspect symptom, signaling the Appassionato. With Fauré, even the prestos dawdle, and the spinning girls themselves are strolling, not walking.[35] How little the spinning girls in act 1 of *Pénélope* resemble Mendelssohn's, with their demonic *moto perpetuo.* Not that Fauré has no prestos whatsoever: the fifth *Impromptu,* which runs like whitewater, is really the School of Velocity and perpetual movement.

But the true Fauréian movement is the Barcarolle, at once animated and peaceful. The second *Valse-caprice* itself, despite its brisk tempo, has something distant and dreamy about it, in short, something nocturnal, which allies it with the Barcarolle's nonchalance and constitutes bergamasque comedy. One needs infinite tact to get it right, this peaceful speed, just as one needs infinite tact to capture the anapests of strolling with friends, a pace that is neither dragging nor hurrying, and to play them without jostling or rushing. The traces of these anapests can be found in all sorts of bergamasque pieces: in the Agnus Dei of the *Requiem*, in "Clair de lune" from *Fêtes galantes*, in the Serenade for cello op. 98, the *Jardin de Dolly*, and the flute-player interlude from act 1 of *Pénélope*.

Tact is no less critical in capturing certain nuances of performance that are, in themselves, contradictory, notably the resonant pianissimo—a pianistic tour de force frequently demanded by Debussy and Albeniz.[36] The same is true of the muted forte, whose role in Fauré's sixth *Nocturne* (or Georges Migot's) is similar to that played by the resonant pianissimo in Debussy's piano preludes or in Albeniz's *Iberia*. These two nuances of dynamics amount to the same thing and meet each other at "mezzo forte," but their purposes are opposite. The resonant pianissimo is half-revealed mystery, in which the forte played with the soft pedal is attenuated radiance, intensity muffled by a mute. The deadened forte is to the pianissimo with enhanced resonance as allegretto is to andantino: they meet in the same, moderate speed, but the former is a slowed-down allegro, where the latter is an accelerated andante.

And the same thing is true of tonalities in equal-temperament tuning and their enharmonic synonyms: D-flat and C-sharp, G-flat and F-sharp; they coincide physically on the keys of the instrument, but spelling with flats corresponds to a wish to shield, while spelling with sharps is an unveiling. A distinction has been made; it is physically inaudible, but the imperceptible differential, the unknowable something, is equally critical in the opposition of dusk and dawn.

This is the diaphora engendered by intention, and it is engendered by what is imponderable, indefinable, and unrecognizable in temporality per se. It has to do with two inverse motions, which are as a result not comparable to one another: one is the already-nocturnal, inclining toward sleep, dreams, and exquisite pleasure; the other inclines toward day and the

Op. 46. Clair de Lune

Andantino quasi allegretto

Op. 56 Jardin de Dolly

Andantino

Pénélope 1, 4

Allegretto molto moderato

Op. 48. Agnus Dei

Op. 98. Sérénade pour Piano et Violoncello

Allegro moderato

Music Example 3. Bergamasque works by Fauré

morning's hard labors. The quantity of available light is identical; the sun stands at the same point, at the horizon; but the quality of light in each case is utterly, completely different. In the same way, the same physical sonority or tonality possesses an entirely different quality when arrayed in flat signs with their dying light than it does when arrayed in sharp signs with their nascent dawn, the sharp-key synonym that represents emergence into light. These two forms of tonal illumination are never psychologically interchangeable and can never be equivalent. Fauré's sixth *Nocturne* is inconceivable in C-sharp major. Thus with Fauré, as with Balakirev, Albeniz, and Janáček, there is an entire poetics of flat-key sonorities, which acts to filter light, giving expression to the penumbra, the half-tint, half-day. If D-flat major gives voice to Fauré's nocturnal intentions—like the muted forte—then the resonant pianissimo translates the Debussyian mystery, the enigma of noon: the furtive advent of innuendo just as great, meridinal day reaches its zenith. Debussy's sixth *Épigraphe antique*, or Albeniz's marvelous *Jerez*, are wholly enveloped, are awash in this ambient quiet resonance (*dolce ma sonoro*), at once vibrant and moribund, intense and clouded over.

But how to get resonant plenitude and imperceptible murmur at the same time, simultaneous legato and staccato? Or bring brilliant sound and silence together in the same sonority? Give voice to an indefinable timbral quality, where (according to Verlaine) "inconclusiveness marries precision," where blur seems paradoxically clear? Properly speaking, this paradoxical *coincidentia oppositorum* is impossible; properly speaking, there is no simple, unequivocal recipe that will result in a resonant sotto voce, the *sotto voce ma sonoro* that lends an evasive precision to the staccatos in "The Interrupted Serenade" and in *El Albaicin*, with their dissolved and fluent aridity. And one would say as much of the Fauréian *forte con sordina*, muffled radiance, where the same ambiguity has been turned inside out. How can one simultaneously speak loudly

Music Example 4. Fauré, sixth *Nocturne; Offertoire* for piano

and speak with a lowered voice? That forte and piano occur in succession makes sense. But can they coexist? With Fauré (for instance, in the *Requiem*), one often finds crescendos that end with a piano, the phalanx that opens up but stops short at "*p*," a paradoxical nuance and its paradoxical sign. It evokes suppressed force, depth, and reticence. Once more, interrupted inflation—understatement—is the breathing heart of the *Offertoire*, and in the sixth *Nocturne* as well (see music ex. 4).[37]

In the *Fantasy for Flute*, one senses waves of false crescendos that rise and fall in turn. In the realm of harmonic resolution, motion through the circle of fifths—seeming modulation that returns to the initial key after having played at escaping toward far-off horizons—gives expression to impulse held back and reined in. In the same way, in the realm of dynamic nuance, the false crescendo that ends with a piano gives expression to force subject to control, contained. There is a certain beauty in not doing all one can, not revealing one's worth all at once.

The deflated crescendo is a paradox, but the forte con sordina is, strictly speaking, unplayable since forte and piano

have become simultaneous. If one has to put down the soft
pedal, what is the use of playing loudly? And if forte is to be
present, what is the use of muffling it? The point is that the
forte deadened by the mute on the one hand, and mezzo-forte
on the other, do not amount to the same thing, do not have
the same quality of sound, or timbre, or flavor. In the opening
measures of the sixth *Nocturne*, the contest between frustrated
force and the mute that suppresses it unleashes the mystery
that is power held back. The phobia about the sostenuto
pedal, the fear of rubato and rallentando: earlier, I described
these as symptoms of musical understatement. And I can repeat the point here. Performers are confronted with several
paradoxes: to produce a sonority that is at once powerful and
vaporous; to reveal while effacing, unveil while arraying, affirm while denying, say "no" and "yes" at the same time.
Properly speaking, the means to realize these paradoxes physically do not exist. Imponderable touch, a left hand that sings,
a weightless one, iron fingers gloved in velvet: would any of
these solve the acoustic paradox entailed by a sonority in
which precision has chosen to be vague, or density likes to
appear negligible?

These bass lines are at once thickly indistinct and articulated with great delicacy, but perhaps this nimbleness—the
constant flight *between*—is *cosa mentale*, a thing of the mind
(see music ex. 5). In the sixth and seventh *Nocturnes*, the spac-
ing of the voices, the way the chords are attacked, the low bass
notes that at times occur off the beat, will explain in part the
crepuscular vagueness, the defining mark of aristocratic nonchalance, which conceals rhythmic rigor just as it hides the
power that is so admirably held back in an economy of truly
nocturnal pianism. And still: that is inadequate. Archangel
hands would be needed to convey this ambivalence, to produce
a sonority that is simultaneously affirmed and refused, just as a
quasi-miraculous power of divination would be needed to hit
upon the untroubled acoustic velocity of allegretto between the

Music Example 5. Fauré, fifth *Nocturne*, sixth *Nocturne*

extremes of presto and adagio. At the very least, one would
need a kind of celestial musicality to understand an art that
combines bitter violence in *Prométhée* with suave languor in
Roses d'Ispahan. It is, in effect, in the spiritual movement to
performance that these irrational contradictions are actually
resolved, and the bergamasque allegretto, the nocturnal trans-
lucence of D-flat major, will set forth their ineffable mystery,
the mystery of innocence. Innocence: it is limpid obscurity
and surface depth.

Musical reality is situated neither in literature, nor in ideology, nor technique, nor biographical anecdotes. But, on the
other hand, it *is* situated in all these things, at least a little,
and more, in a thousand other things that one cannot enu-
merate. I am not here to find handholds in music, to have
something to say about it, nor to confer a pseudoconsistency
on ultimate inconsistency by means of analogies taken at face
value. On the contrary, I am following Plotinus: in multiply-
ing and destroying the metaphors one by one, the mind will
be subtly deflected towards the Platonists' "great *matheme*."

And in this case, there is hope: in calling upon all the arts, all the analogies drawn from all possible sensations, our minds will be drawn toward some intimation of the almost-nothing of music. This does not entail defining this almost-nothing, or feeling it with our fingers, but, rather, in remaking something along with its maker, take part in his or her processes, re-create what he or she created. Caught in the poetic momentum that will have been set in motion, the subordinate re-creator, fertilized, becoming a poet in turn, will someday reproduce—who knows?—the initial act, the original poetic condition where works of art improvise themselves into existence.

But we must acknowledge that for this purpose simple listening, or performing per se, is far more effective than the most striking intellectual insights. Listening to music creates a state of grace in the blink of an eye, where long pages of poetic metaphors would not suffice. As irrationalist as this conclusion may seem, we need to accede to it. Listening gives us a glimpse of ineffable Kitezh, unexpectedly reveals Kitezh (which is concealed from the eye, but not the ear), and transports us instantaneously into the esoteric Kitezh of enchantment, of the Charm. From the outset, listening transgresses the limits of intellectual speculation, poetic as the latter might be. Since, when words are no longer worth saying, what can one do, except sing?

WISDOM AND MUSIC

Here is one way to explain all music's fundamental inevidence, the element of ambiguity, the debatable aspect in whatever certainties it offers us. When "works" exist only in a parlous sense, how could the objective value of such works not be dependent upon the author's sincerity, which is in turn an ambiguous, moral quality? And how would this value not be dependent upon inexhaustible spiritual conditioning, on a personal context in which *our* own emotions and our entire past have been enlisted?

But in all this, what then becomes of the unambiguous criteria that aesthetics aspires to define? We need to come to its defense: not-obvious music, which is the modernist art par excellence, hardly exists and exists by surprise, and that very little is needed for it to cease existing entirely (this proves the absolute, annihilating force of bad music). Like *Anima* (in Claudel's parable), blameless Fevroniya stops singing as soon as the doctors look at her. Music is a charm, made of nothing, insisting upon nothing, and perhaps it is nothing—at least for those who expect to discover something, something palpable and unequivocal. Like an iridescent soap bubble that quivers and glows for a few seconds in the sunlight, music collapses the moment you touch it and does not exist, except as a highly dubious, fugitive exaltation in an opportune moment. Music is inconsistent, almost nonexistent, the site where thought disaggregates and becomes nocturnal, a ravishing ambiguity and the exquisite, deceptive mirage of the instant, and music is like everything precarious, pleasurable, and irreversible, like the hint of the past carried on a fugitive perfume, a memory of childhood long gone. Music makes us into absurd and passionate creatures. We hold dear something that lasts only a second, or happens only once, and we do so fervently, infinitely, as if ardor alone could imprison a thing without substance, and cause it to endure. Even though music's Charm can be replayed, it is as precious to us as childhood and innocence, or as cherished fellow-creatures fated to die. The Charm is labile and fragile, and our presentiments of its obsolescence lend poetic melancholia to the state of grace it has engendered.

Does music make us wise? Wisdom only arises in a climate in which serenity and the perennial are conjoined; wisdom is not just coextensive with life in its entirely but also makes us calm, eases our anxiety. In this case, it would seem, music does not confer wisdom but only half-wisdom: though music's effects are enduring, they are confusing; and when music is reassuring, that reassurance and the serenity it engenders is generally ephemeral. With music, spiritual tranquility and the perennial state are never given to us in the same package. Should one choose seriousness without serenity, or rather swift serenity without the serious aspect of total engagement? If music is serious, then it lacks tranquilizing effect. No, in this sense music does not make those who practice it particularly wise.

Rather, music invokes an unreasonable existence, a bit orgiastic, consciousness made frenetic, ravaged by tragedy, or deliria, prey to backward-looking nostalgia or to the wrathful storms of passion. Intoxication is not wisdom. Is it wise to encourage human concupiscence, indulgence in unhappiness? Scriabin's *Poème tragique* will not confer imperturbability upon anxious men; nor will the *Symphonie pathétique* render us apathetic. It is well known that Tolstoy accused music of awakening everything disturbing, immodest, and illicit in human hearts. If music invades one's entire life, it is only to confuse and upend it; while conversely if music is calming, it becomes no more than a local, superficial divertissement. Does this mean that music can pacify and sedate but cannot be serious?

Certainly once music renounces all expression of tragic human fate, then it can provide us with harmonious pacing, a momentary stylization of existence. In place of physical sleep, it procures peace of the soul, at least for a moment. Aristotle speaks of purged emotion, παθημάτων κάθαρσις, and this flows, as if naturally, from Fauré's music. In this sense, the *Requiem, Le plus doux chemin,* and *Ruisseau* (for women's chorus) are lessons in equanimity: thus a "gentle feeling of deep calm" is poured into us, is promised to nocturnal hearts. This is the benison of musical catharsis: the mind that disputes endlessly will be liberated; one passes from the state of

Music Example 6. Peter Ilich Chaikovsky, "Dumka"

war to peace, care to innocence. But isn't that wisdom's usual effect? Music makes a man into his own friend, for a few instants. But more: it may reconcile him with all nature. In Ravel's *L'Enfant et les Sortilèges*, the animals are charmed when their hearts are moved and are reconciled with the Child, just as the wild bear, in Rimsky's *Kitezh*, will lick Fevroniya's hand; the Child takes pity on the injured squirrel, just as Fevroniya bends over the wound of her companion the reindeer.

Still, can one speak of wisdom when this serenity has no tomorrow? If equanimity of the soul does not endure beyond the instant, is it equanimity of the soul to begin with? First let me make this clear: music, even with its furies and its cadenzas senza tempo, is always stylized time; but this time is no more than a provisional suspension of amorphous, disjointed time, the prosaic and tumultuous time of daily existence. Stylized time is a temporal interruption of unstylized duration; but it is also temporary. Better still: stylized time is experienced in the present as if it were an eternal Now, but this eternity, if one can put it this way, is a provisional eternity:

not the definitive, literal nontemporality promised us by eschatological immortality, but a scornful eternity that lasts only a quarter-hour, sonata eternity. What is a sonata, something set apart within that sonata of all sonatas, the hyper-drama called human life? What is a sonata within the interval of, and in relation to, the chaotic continuousness of existence? Alas, exemplary time in four movements is only a temporary lapse, an enchanted but limited time, a marvel of a delay, and is as nicely circumscribed within our biographies as the statue on its pedestal or the painting it its frame. A musician clears a "*moment musicale*"[38] within our laborious daily occupations, where wait-and-see duration is no longer felt. But for the transcendent superconscience, this lovely moment will end. And more still: even in this "moment," the musical-ness of music will often be due to an even briefer conjunction, the briefest instant within a brief moment, an opportune minute, one beat of a single measure—like the ravishing chord in Chabrier's *Sulamite*, like the captivating harmonic sequence in Chaikovsky's *Dumka*, or the Gregorian cadence at the end of Fauré's fifth piano prelude. The Charm hangs on the imponderable musical-ness of a brief occasion, a lightning strike of an event.

But can one install wisdom on the seat of this delicate, imperceptible point in an ephemeral instant?

It will not be enough to reply, with Hans Christian Andersen, that the ephemeral day, infinitely full of instants, equals the centenarian's long life in intense richness. For a human being's duration precedes and survives the "moments musicales," and these enchanted moments, even if they resonate in memory and are thus prolonged, tend to annul themselves eventually within the mediocrities of Becoming. Philosophical reason no longer transports us to the eternal; rather, it limits itself to conceiving of things *under the aspect* of eternity, *sub quadam specie*. In that reason at least entails a progressive eternalization, at least lends life dignity and manner, and a properly philosophical style that transforms the totality of existence, this philosophical style is nothing other than wisdom. Wisdom that does not exceed the limits of a single afternoon, or last longer than the length of a record, is not wisdom at all—if wisdom is diathesis, a permanent manner of being that is capable of transforming a human being.

Rather, this brief wisdom is the wisdom of the Ephemeral, wisdom in midget size. True wisdom, just as it is independent of changes in the weather, must be independent of the lunatic caprices of mood: the Humoresques, the Capriccios, and the Fantasies are not its business. How could a passing whim take the place of wisdom? How could "fugitive impressions" (so Prokofiev's *Mimolyotnosti* must be understood) be consoling in any lasting way? Thus it comes to pass that feelings of deep calm are reduced to frivolous, polite indifference, to the indifference of those amiable "moments musicales," and that eternal peace becomes in effect fifteen minutes' truce. A pastime hovering just above existence, or (as the epigraph of the *Valses nobles et sentimentales* has it) the "exquisite pleasure of a futile pursuit"—no, there is nothing of deep calm in all that! One can nonetheless wager that Ravel, with his secretly passionate nature, is showing a flash of humor with a glove thrown down to Romantic excess, and that music, for him, was never—never—a "Déjeuner sur l'herbe," the al fresco lunch of a pastoral afternoon.

What remains true is that the intermittent character of the métier, in the case of music, resonates with the momentary, exceptional character of the evasion. The creative act is discontinuous; and our sacred moments of delectation and ecstasy are no less so. Music, like theatrical performances of tragedies, never completely loses its regional character, the hint of the divertimento and the happy illusion. Chausson's Symphony in B-flat, with its metaphysical anxieties, Chaikovsky's profound third symphony, with its fateful trumpets, are strictly speaking no more "serious" than a suite by Scar-

latti or Cimerosa. And the lives of musicians often affirm this
fundamental insularity of the work of art: it is often the case
that their sublime occupations stand out in sharp contrast to
the meanness of their preoccupations, and that their lives
seem little affected, warmed, illuminated, or transfigured—
strangely so—by the glow of the happy musical moments.
For music, just as it does not make us wiser, does not make us
better;[39] that is, music does not have the power to chronically
or constantly ameliorate our moral existence, and a life in
music does not necessarily imply excellence in the realm of
virtue. Why doesn't singular virtuosity, or talent itself, operate
in tandem with the micro-psyche?

Music is not always something that one can rethink. In
principal, and literally, the magic half-hour we call Sonata or
String Quartet will always have no tomorrow, and—until the
next performance—disappears without leaving a trace; it is as
if the work had ceased to exist between the moments when
one brings it into being in playing it. And afterwards? That is
the essence of Tolstoy's question. Will the Sonata glide over us
without improving us? Should we be indebted to it for some
superficial exaltation, which will have no lasting repercus-
sions? Will nothing follow it, nothing at all? Is it really written
that this state of grace will be without lasting consequences?
Must one admit that enchantment runs out?

"LAETITIAE COMES"

Truly, the musical operation, like the "poetic" initiative, is
nascent action, and this is why it deserves to be called a
"Charm" (in Henri Bremond's sense) and not "magic."[40] A
charm is magic in the figural sense, a mystical transaction, not
a black-magical one. Like dance, which is pointless motion, or
drama, which is fictive action, like all the tragic and comic
gestures, epic, poetic, Romanesque, even ritual gestures, music
is an action in the process of beginning, and the concert hall

is as much an unreal space, as much an imaginary microcosm, as the theater or the amphitheater: this space—theater
or circus—is consecrated space, art encircled by a ludic wall,
its very closure sets the enchanted island of the chimeras apart
from the ocean of serious action.

Tolstoy, as we saw, gets incensed about this: music, whether
march, dance, berceuse, or mass, is an unfinished process that
does not reach any goal; music does not prepare us for great
things that are just around the corner, for, alas, the great
things are eternally pending and never manifest themselves. Is
there not reason for disappointment here? Music accentuates
and punctuates labor, but it is not itself this labor; music accompanies processions without being a procession, and ig-
nites the warriors' ardor without replacing battle, and never
in itself causes the enemy to beat a retreat. Always secondary
and symbolic, music is ineffective accompaniment, a friend
for frivolous days, holidays; servant to the serious life. It appears that music does not keep its promises. But what did it
promise us? And why, if you will, should an action left incomplete be tantamount to an aborted action? Music is not an
elliptical gesture or wasted action: singing is a way of *doing*
that is absolutely original and cannot be understood (except
metaphorically) on the model of such processes as labor or
action.

Therefore, it would an injustice to cry foul or claim "deception," or complain that the enchantment would better be
named disenchantment. Certainly, it is true that prosaic time,
which frees us of enchantment once we leave the closed space
of singing, is not fooling the dupe—rather, it strips him of his
deceptions. Serious words, as well as musical noise, disabuse
the person so abused by musical intoxication, and disabuse
him far more radically than Rimsky-Korsakov's dawns, where
those made mad by nocturnal phantasmagorias are brought
to their senses, even more radically the sleepwalkers who are
sobered up by Satie's matitudinal music.

But this is a critical point: "enchantment" does not "deceive"—that is: it fools only those who aspire to angelic status. For there is no such thing as a miraculous cure or a perpetual ecstasy, and midnight's truth is no more true than noon's; moonlight intoxication is after all necessarily temporary. To imagine a state of grace that continually refreshed the long droughts of our being would only imagine a chimera. This is something without sense, an unimaginable, almost superhuman idea, like the idea of a "continuous state of an instantaneous point," a kind of contradiction *in-adjecto*, as contradictory as the dream of an eternal celebration, which negates the idea of celebration per se. Because the long working days make possible the very idea of a holiday, and the mediocre, empirical interval makes the blessed instant an escape and a clear victory over an alternative. Thus inspiration is not a state of grace; it is a "point" of grace, a fine, extreme point where the soul, for a few instants, ends up on top of itself. All divine, sublime things that are vouchsafed to human beings in brief glimpses have this same nature, at once dazzling and dubious. For us, the Absolute itself is a vanishing apparition. Musical rapture is an escape from immanence— but it also does not breach that wall; it merely makes an opening, similar to the opening cleared within our human condition by an innocent, highly fragile emotion, caritas. By virtue of that sharp point, a soul enchanted by music, the almost-nothing, escapes its finitude. Most futile of all futile things, ματαιότης ματαιοτήτων (vanity of vanities), glint of a glint! Expecting to become immortal listeners at an eternal concert, human beings end, after the celebration, as finite beings once again, just as a composer, who is never an unflagging genius, will sink and become an imitation of himself, a mere continuation of his beginning. Wise Fevroniya, almost nonexistent, does not confer wisdom upon those who listen to her: for she is the opposite of a thamaturge and in any case does not bring the dead back to life. But she does better: in her enigmatic smile, in her strange blue eyes, in a flash, we read the only secret of the absolute that human beings can access, and this celestial instant fulfils us more than years of patient labor ever will. Like Fevroniya, the most futile of futile things does not quiet my soul for more than an instant: in fact, it does not *engender* quiet. It is moreover the accompaniment, not the cause, of my serenity. In the end, its powers are not physical, but spiritual: for music does not make miracles, does not cure plagues or snakebite; music cannot make grain grow, or rain fall. Music does not change owls into princesses or bring back a departed lover; music does not literally make others submissive or assuage their desires. Chopin's *Berceuse* is not good for literally putting little children to sleep, nor will Fauré's Barcarolles help gondolas glide over the water, nor will Polonaises lead actual squadrons as they march, and Valses are not to be danced to. Federico Mompou links together six *Charmes* into six incantations, and among them the first is "to assuage suffering," the last "to summon joy." Suffering, in effect, is more put to sleep than cured, and doubtless it is in this sense that music acts, as Aristotle puts it, φαρμαχείας χάριν, "as a medicine."[41] And as for joy, music is not its cause, but its companion.

So I would prefer to say (with Vermeer), *laetitiae comes, medecina dolores*, the words inscribed on the lid of the clavichord in *The Music Lesson*, the silent music made by a girl-musician of silence. Music does not lend us the blessings of the gods, but as the companion of happiness, *laetitiae comes*, and as the cure for sorrow, a consolation in affliction, it can rekindle a spark of joy, for an instant, and make each human being a demi-god. If joy and philosophy are children of the same happy instant, would we not be inclined to say, paraphrasing Plato's *Phaedo*, that philosophy is a sort of supreme music, ὡς φιλοσοφίας οὔσης μεγίστης μουσικῆς? Even reduced to a deceiving, innocent instance, music is still worth the trouble. It reveals to us our own profound joys, our un-

known joys, the ones we never recognized, concealed as they
were by care and hidden by petty emotions. Like Aristotle's
songs of purification, music gives us joy without shame,
χαρὰν ἀβλαβῆ, "harmless joy."[42]

Thus musical enchantment recompenses those who have
renounced musical incantation. Maurice Ravel (in *L'Enfant et
les Sortilèges*) and Manuel De Falla (in *El amor brujo*) associated incantation with enchantment: but the latter word remains nonetheless the last word. In Ravel's opera, the evil
magic vanishes after a single word, "Mama," and peace reigns
in the garden, soothing the trees' enraged groans and the animal furor. This is the same celestial "enchantment" that
breaks the evil curse put on the prince, in Ravel's *Ma mère
l'oye* (in "Entretiens de la Belle et la Bête"), and changes the
Beast into a Prince who is more beautiful that love itself. In
the same way, the morning bells at the end of *El amor brujo*
celebrate the kiss that the Gypsy at last receives from Carmelo:
thus enchantment conjures away bewitchment. Love the enchanter exorcises the sorcery of Love the magician. Candelas—transfixed by black magic and intoxicated by all those
magical brews—receives the *consolamentum* of truth and
leaves the magic circle that had held him in thrall. The death
potion is transformed into an elixir of life, a fortifying cor-
dial. The unknowable something engendered by love-sickness
becomes joyous fervor, and freedom savored in full daylight,
the unknowable something that is divine. The Charm succeeds black magic, and the ineffable the unsayable. Among all
the philosophical and alchemical transmutations that make
metamorphosis possible, none is more miraculous than the
transfiguration of an inspired heart: "sing, bells; sing, joy; my
love draws near."

f o u r

MUSIC AND SILENCE

"*In silence*": *the last words that appear in Jean* Wahl's treatise on metaphysics. To apply these words to music—under the pretext that music, being born of silence, withdraws into silence—would perhaps mean confusing metaphysics with the metaphorical, and disfigure the ideas of a singular poet-philosopher. Nonetheless, the eschatological model is tempting: imagine the blank backdrop, the fabric upon which the noises of life and nature and music ultimately inscribe themselves. Just as experience (according to certain sensualist and substantialist epistemologies) carves ornamental signs into the tabula rasa, into original nonconsciousness, and just as the painter's brush deposits the picturesque wildness of color on a colorless and uniform canvas, so the unwritten page that is silence, original nothingness, gradually fills up with tumult. In this case, it is the world of noises and sounds that would constitute a parenthesis in the backdrop of silence, and that would emerge from an ocean of silence, like a ray of light that illuminates homogenous space, the black void of the χώρα (chora), for a few instants.

This is the impression made by the tolling of the discordant, arhythmic bells in Louis Vuillemin,[1] which come from a distance, and usher in the evening above the open window, among the ribbons of cloud. Noise in this case is connected to human presence, which—as loud as it may be with its cackling and shrieking and trumpets and shrill rattles—is a sigh barely audible in the eternal silence of infinite space. This presence, like civilization itself, must affirm and reaffirm itself without end, by constant vigilance and self defense, to resist the invasion of nothingness. And just as abandoned places will become overgrown, covered in wild grass little by little, from the moment we relax our vigilance, just as the most animated cities will disappear under the earth if human beings do not constantly maintain them and reclaim them from the sands, so even the most clamorous earthly reputation, sooner or later—that is to say, ultimately—will end up lost in the oceanic immensity of endless time. Oblivion, which is a kind of silence, will eventually submerge it; only a few distant memories will remain floating, and they in turn are attenuated little by little, and finally disappear completely.

If existence—which we suppose to be fragile, superficial, and provisional—tends asymptotically toward nothingness, then music, gradually exhausting all possible combinations of sounds, tends inexorably toward silence. More generally, noise accompanies change and signals mutability, the shifting of one state into another, which occurs in time. Effective movement or spatial displacement—the simplest form of change—produces an acoustic vibration in the air and is realized in consequence as disorder or chaos, acoustic agitation and cacophony. Bare time, abstract time, is silent time, but Becoming is filled with events and occurrences, fitted out with concrete contents fashioned from noise. Noises succeed one another and sounds imply continuation, imply it intensely, like the notes a singer sustains and extends with vibrato: time is their natural dimension. And conversely, death is a form of stagnation, which, arresting the process of Becoming as it does all movement, forces loquacious events to fall into silence. The living, as everyone knows, have a superstitious habit of speaking softly in the presence of the dead, even though one cannot disturb a corpse and though this would actually be the proper moment to raise one's voice, loudly and vociferously. "Careful! Now we need to speak softly," says Arkel in *Pelléas* act 5, in the tongue of Michelangelo. Thus it is the living who fall in step with a lethal eternity and its quietude, where nothing will happen again, or survive, or become: history and with it the entire fracas of event has forever deserted this new eon, so perfectly void of all occurrence.

Life floats like a raft on this great volume of silence, a silence that makes all human noise a bit precarious, and makes the enchanted island that is art so precious. Poetry is a sonorous island in an ocean of prose; or (to evoke other images), the living oasis of music and poetry is as if lost in muteness, in the immense desert of prosaic existence. Just as architecture is the artifice that fills space with formal volumes, cubes and towers, just as painting populates a monochromatic surface with color—that is, with the positive polarity, the diversity inherent in multicolored splashes—so music and poetry animate time, superficially, by means of rhythm as well as mellifluous noise. Music stands out from silence and has need of silence in the same way that life has need of death, and thought—according to Plato's *Sophist*—has need of nonbeing. As something similar to a work of art, life is an animated, limited construction that stands out against lethal infinity; and music, as something similar to life—as a melodious construction, magic duration, an ephemeral adventure, and brief encounter—is isolated, between beginning and end, in the immensity of nonbeing.

Thus, one can distinguish between anterior silence and consequent silence, which are to one another as alpha to omega. The silence-before and the silence-after are no more mutually "symmetric" than beginning and end, or birth and death, within the irreversible unspooling of time.[2] Symmetry is a spatial image. A double silence bathes Debussy's music,

which floats, entire, on a peaceful, silent sea. *E silentio, ad* Music
silentium, per silentium: from silence to silence, across silence: and
this could be the motto of Debussy's music, since silence suf- Silence
fuses it, in each of its parts. If Debussy's music is thus foreshortened cosmogony, a recapitulation of the world's history, 133
then *Pelléas et Mélisande* is in turn a foreshortening of the
foreshortened. The first act begins with a mysterious noise
in the lowest registers, behind which one can make out the
theme associated with Golaud, dull and faraway, galloping
rhythm, and soon Mélisande's theme as well: fate plots the
meeting of two unknown figures in the forest, with two
themes at its side. This silence is a precursor, an advance runner: silence as annunciation of the storm.

But it does not always announce a tragedy: in general, it is
rather a prophetic silence, prophesying that something will
appear. This is the silence that suddenly comes into being just
before a concert, when the conductor's baton suppresses the
cacophony of instruments and, with the first beat of the first
measure, releases a harmonious symphonic torrent. And to
the degree that initial silence is a promise, or a threat, terminal silence designates instead the nothingness to which life
returns: music born of silence returns to silence. *Pelléas* is
encompassed by the two silences. At the end of act 5, a Mélisande without substance disappears into a murmur: that
which was almost nonexistent stops existing at all. "And the
rest is silence."[3] There is nothing more, nothing, as at the end
of Debussy's song "Colloque sentimental," where, on a frigid
night, solitude and wind carry off the last words spoken by a
pair of spectral lovers. Listen to the silence at the end of act 5
of *Pelléas*, silence "more silent than the soul," than death,
more than all the most silent things there are. In the steppes
of central Asia, an interminable ennui where a caravan, escorted by Russian soldiers, winds across the plains, some harmonious singing draws nearer, fades into distance, and finally
loses itself, reabsorbed into immensity. The obstinate horizon-

tal monotone of a dominant pedal dies out into gray uniformity; nothing remains but sand and silence.[4] The lumbering of a chariot crossing the steppe expires at the horizon.[5] The last brass bands at the festival (in Debussy's "Fêtes"), the last sighs of the bagpipe (in Bartók), the last sobs of the mandolin (in Musorgsky) dissipate in silence.[6] *On doute—la nuit— J'écoute—Tout fuit—Tout passe—L'espace—Efface—Le bruit.* Alain admired these lines from Victor Hugo's *Djinns*, since it is gray desert sand, like Siberia's solitude, that submerges all noise.[7] In all reality, "one hears nothing more."[8]

For this reason, the works of Franz Liszt, noisy with heroism, with epic pomp and triumphal glare, find themselves gradually invaded by silence with approaching old age. A maternal silence enters into their every pore; long pauses come to interrupt recitatives, great voids, empty staves and measures that rarify each note, detach it from all others. The music of the *Messe basse*, the *Valses oubliées*, the *Gondole funèbre*, and the symphonic poem *Du berceau à la tombe*, becomes increasingly discontinuous. Nothingness, like the encroaching sand, invades the melody, desiccates its verve. Could one not say that silence exists before, after, and during? At once on both flanks and in the interval between?

But noise's relation to silence could also be conceived in the opposite way. According to eschatology—a science that considers ins and outs, envisages the beginning of beginnings and the end of all ends—noise is the island in the sea, the oasis or secret garden in the sands. If one considers the empirical fact of continuation, however, then silence instead would constitute the interruption or the discontinuous pause within the continuity of incessant sound. Noise is not suspended silence, but silence is noise than has ended, and the suspension of continuity. Previously, it was change itself—living, increasing diversity—that stood out from boredom's uniform oceanography and that troubled a preexisting and subterranean continuousness. Silence was the backdrop suspended under

Being. But now, it is noise that constitutes a sonorous foundation, suspended under silence. And this continuous pedal
point, this obstinate fundamental bass skewered by momentary silence is indeed more imperceptible than the sound of
the sea: it lasts our whole life and accompanies all we experience, fills our ears from the time we are born to the moment
we die. As an interruption, a momentary lacuna that mars the
noisy animation of Becoming, silence blossoms through voids
that interrupt a perpetual din.

Now I am calling it a "din": but is it not what I called
"silence" before? In the first instance, man as a creature of
distractions isolated himself on his little islet of sonority to
beguile away the anguish of solitude and the silence that deforms being—like a traveler lost in the night, who talks and
laughs as loudly as possible to persuade himself that he is not
afraid, who believes that he has put death's phantoms to
flight, thanks to this noisy protective screen. Whereas now
this has been inverted: the person assailed by cacophony, cov-
ering his ears, wants to protect his slip of a silent garden,
shelter his little islet of silence, because henceforth it is silence
that insulates, and not noise. With Debussy, music appears
suddenly out of silence, where music is silence interrupted
or suspended provisionally. But, being entirely *en sourdine*
(muted), Fauré's music instead is itself a form of silence, the
interruption of noise, a silence that breaks into noise: silence
is no longer analogous to nothingness, or a source of anguish,
but is a haven where contemplation co-exists with total quiet.
The "Île joyeuse," to the extent that it is a sonorous island in
an expanse of silence, an island of singing and laughing and
crashing cymbals, is Debussy's chimera, and his alone—because it is for Debussy that jubilation is an enclave smack in
the middle of nonbeing, the parenthesis delimiting nothingness.

Conversely for Fauré, the "Jardin clos," *hortus conclusus* as
the Song of Songs calls it (long before Charles van Leberghe),

could only be a silent garden, the garden of quietude, just as the islet whose mystery in evoked by Rachmaninoff (with Konstantin Balmont) is all silence, all somnolence.[9] This second kind of silence is no longer the limitless ocean or the unformed grayness of the ἄπειρον (infinite); rather, it delimits a well-circumscribed zone within the universal din. Rimsky-Korsakov's operas like to carve out a lake in the midst of their swarming landscapes, and this lake is a zone of solitude and silence: because a lake, which is itself closure, *hortus conclusus*—the silent island—clears a mute space at the heart of the din, just as the island of sonority is isolated within the immensity of silence.[10] So it is that intramusical silences or sighs—the numbered rests, subject to the chronometer, carefully timed—aerate the mass of musical discourse according to the exact rule of the metronome, since music can only breathe when it has the oxygen of silence. Conversely, ambient music filters by osmosis into the middle of an empty measure, to color and qualify silence. Just as microsilences (tiny silences within silence) will aerate endless melody, so restful shores of silence in the middle of universal noisiness constitute a safe haven for repose and reverie. No longer intoxicated with conversation as a means to fill crushing silences at all costs, a human being will now seek out the remaining slicks and shallow pools of silence, that conversation might be cut short. Her goal is no longer distraction, but contemplation.

Because silence is in itself obscure, and an object of dread, it has a function: silence is, after all, not nothingness. Absolute silence, like pure space or bare time, is an inconceivable limit. As Aristotle has already affirmed: οὐ πᾶν τὸ ἀκίνητον ἠρεμεῖ (not everything motionless is at rest).[11] What is immobile is not in repose; this fallow somnolence must conceal some deep activity. Francis Bacon says that silence is the sleep that feeds wisdom; and again, that silence is thought being fermented. Silence is one of the "negative measures" whose positive quality was affirmed by Kant, in opposition to Leibniz (the man of "reduced perceptions"). Nothingness, one might say, has no properties. One nothing cannot be distinguished from another nothing. How could they be distinguished without having qualities or a manner of being; that is, without, at least, being something? Two nothings are only a single, same nothing, a single, same zero. But silence has differential properties: and as a result, this particular nothingness is not *nothing at all*—in other words, it is not (like Parmenides' nothingness) the negation of all being; it is not a nonbeing that totally annihilates or contradicts total being. In Schelling's terms, it would be more μὴ ὄν (potential not being) than οὐκ ὄν (actual not being).

In this instance, nothingness is not the simultaneous negation of all qualities perceptible to the senses; rather, it excludes only a single category of sensation, that of physiological hearing. Flying his true nominalist colors in denouncing the unimaginable absurdity that is "nothingness," Bergson showed that it is impossible to suppress one category of perceptions without reconstituting another in some way. Someone who closes his or her eyes to experience blindness continues to hear; someone who stops his or her ears to experience silence continues to see; and if struck blind and deaf with a single blow, still feels heat, perceives scent, and is granted coenesthesic impressions. Effacing one sense always entails the accession, even the enlivening, of another: plenitude alternates and is displaced but is never radically annihilated. Thus, silence is in turn a relative or partial nothingness and not absolute nothingness.

The most characteristic form of silence is silence brightly illuminated (though such a claim hardly entails denying that there is nocturnal silence as well). But Schelling himself observes that night favors the propagation of sounds, that night exalts sound in the same way that it draws out perfume: the composer who wrote *Les sons et les parfums tournent dans l'air du soir* dedicated the second movement of *Iberia* to the "perfumes of the night." What is true for Debussy is no less true for Albeniz: *Cordoba*, *La Vega*, and Loti's *Le Crépuscule* all evoke darkness made aromatic by carnations and jasmine. In the dark, our auditory perception is enhanced: and, vice versa, it is often in the full daylight that silence is most thunderous.

The silence of noon, which is the nonexistence of the auditory contrasted with a plenitude of optical existence, takes the paradox to its extreme. Noon: in the immobile suspension where all presences coexist, when the sun at its zenith reigns over a universal convocation of beings and beckons them to the siesta, when all things *are*, in actuality, and the shadow line of the virtual no longer creates any effect of contour or relief among them, no longer carves out a zone of innuendo behind them, when time, having arrived at its apogee, when time itself seems to hesitate, then the contrast between clair-voyance (which is plenitude) and silence (which is a void) reaches its point of greatest tension. This meridinal hour, quasi-indifferent, the hour of maximum clarity, the hour that Plato's *Phaedrus* calls μεσημβρία σταθερά (high noon),[12] the hour of Debussyian silence par excellence, the hour when the faun's flute begins to unfold its cantilena: this is the noon that is prelude to that most famous of summer afternoons. At noon, great Pan himself (as Fyodor Ivanovich Tyuchev says) falls asleep among a flock of nymphs, as clouds gather lazily in the sky. Pan's son is Din, and Echo is his fiancée: and even Pan, who made Syrinx, Pan who is the rustling of the springs and the wind's tremors, even he becomes quiet at the exact center of day, when the wind falls asleep. And in order not to disturb Pan's siesta, shepherds stop blowing their rustic in-struments. Schelling spoke marvelously of the "panic silence" that suffuses a countryside that is bombarded with light.

Things fall mute, and their muteness renders their disheart-ening evident-ness paradoxically enigmatic. At the opening of his collection *Impressions d'été* (*Letni dojmy*), Josef Suk allows a perfect triad in B major to vibrate in an almost immobile

state, a fascinating, mid-day drone, as hypnotic as a lullaby. Is
this not panic, static silence, in the form of sustained sound?
The gentle rumor of the *silentium meridianum*? Even Debussy's first symphonic *Nocturne*, "Nuages," is silence bathed
in light.

It is not just that silence is the nothingness of a single category of sensations within the plenitude of all others: silence
itself is never complete. The most ordinary form of silence is
the silence of words. The Ecclesiastes makes a distinction between two "occasions," καιρὸς τοῦ σιγᾶν καὶ καιρὸς τοῦ
λαλεῖν (there is a time to be silent, and a time to speak).
Silence gives us respite from deafening verbal clamor, just as
the word gives respite from overwhelming silence. Silence is
not nonbeing, not at all, since it is simply something *other*
than the noise made by words. If the "loquela," as the
preachers say, is truly the human noise par excellence, then
the muteness that suppresses this noise will be a privileged
form of silence. Music is the silence of words, just as poetry is
the silence of prose. Music, as sonorous presence, fills silence
full, and yet music is itself a manner of silence: there is a
relative silence that consists in a change in the order of noise
being heard, a move from unformed, fortuitous din to sonorous form, just as there is repose that consists in a change
in one's degree of fatigue.

To say, "We need to be quiet," one must already have made
a bit of noise. For example, to say that we do not need to
speak about music, one needs to speak, and philosophy itself,
as a whole, attempts to explain the following: that it is better
not to try to say the unsayable.

Nonetheless, one must make music to obtain silence. Music, which is in itself composed of so many noises, is the silence of all other noises, because as soon as music raises its
voice, it demands solitude and insists that it occupy vibrating
space alone, excluding other sounds. The melodic wave never
shares the place that it insists upon filling up by itself. Music

is a sort of silence, and one needs silence in order to hear music; the one silence is necessary to hear the other, melodious silence. As melodious, measured noise, enchanted noise, music needs to be surrounded by silence. Music imposes silence upon words and their soft purring, that is, upon the most facile and voluble noise of all, the noise of idle chatter. Noise is left speechless, the better to hear the incantation. Presences can coexist in space, but in the sounding succession of noises, simultaneity is mutually disturbing and uncoordinated voices will mutually disturb one another. Those voices require either polyphonic synchronization or the precaution of silence, which isolates music from cackling conversation.

And yet music, forcing human beings to be quiet, is also imposing something on their voices: the sustained, faintly solemn intonations of singing. Singing does away with telling, or saying. Singing is a way of being quiet. Federico Mompou gave the name *Musica callada* to a suite of nine small "pieces" that I would have called nine "silences," in which the *soledad sonora* of St. John of the Cross is given a chance to sing. Music rises up out of silence, divine music. With Ravel, when the crickets' chirping stops ("one hears nothing more"), vast chords ascend in the night sky; when pointless conversations cease, music (like supplication) will populate the empty space. With this, music buoys up the heavy weight of logos, loosens the devastating hegemony of the word, and prevents the human genus from becoming overidentified with the spoken alone. In Ravel, the "musician of silence" described by Mallarmé assumed earthly form.[13]

Furthermore, music is not just discourse fallen silent. The "silence of music" is itself a constituent part of audible music. It is not just that music needs words to fall silent so that it might sing: silence also inhabits and dampens audible music. Laconic tendencies, reticence, and the pianissimo are like silences within silence. In effect, brachylogy—brevity, concision of diction—is a form of silence in the music of Satie or

Mompou. The *pièce brève* is a silence not in that it emerges from silence, but indirectly, in that it expresses a desire to retighten the grip, a will to concentration. Concision harbors the wish to disturb silence as little as possible. Thus *reticence* must be considered a privileged form of silence: for the silence that is no longer "tacit" or simply "taciturn," but "reticent," is a special form of silence, the one that arises quite suddenly, at the brink of mystery, at the threshold of the ineffable, where the vanity and impotence of words have become all too obvious. Reticence is a refusal to go on and on, resistance to the practice of inertia, to the ease of oratorical automatism. It says "No!" to the temptations of verbosity and to loquacious puffery, and in this is a costly and wholly astonishing choice: for freedom. Just as "will"—a semantic negative, in the sense of something imposed upon others, or as desire—can in fact be more positive than "consent," so *not saying* is often more persuasive than *saying everything*. There is a sort of mental reserve in the face of the inexpressible, which goes beyond anger suppressing its threat, beyond innuendo (which prefers to insinuate or imply), and this reserve flows not so much from a sense of discouragement as from an intimation of poetry, from the glimpse of the mystery.

According to Plotinus, this is the mystic ecstasy of the sage, who, having rejected all forms of discourse, πάντα λόγον ἀφείς, "putting away all reasoning,"[14] no longer dares to offer a single word, οὐδ᾽ ἂν ὅλως φθέγξασθαι δύναιτο, "nor is he able to utter a word."[15] Music in its entirety—in that it causes words to be quiet, commands the cessation of noise—could thus be the silence of discourse. And music itself, as we have seen, sometimes expresses itself allusively, half-speaking, not at all exhaustively. Plotinus's suspension of logos and Debussy's interrupted serenade are two ways to strangle eloquence, two forms of human propriety in the face of the untellable. What do they tell us, these moments where implications are left hanging? They are saying, Finish this your-

Music Example 7. Louis Aubert, *Crépuscules d'Automne* no. 3, "Silence"

selves because I have said too much. Like Arkel, they whisper that the human soul is very, very silent; "she needs silence, now."[16] In opposition to logos with its surfeit of eloquence, which wants to say everything and claims to speak of everything, they elect to suggest, to advise us gently that we should leave in silence, σιωπήσαντας δεῖ ἀπελθεῖν, "we must go away in silence."[17]

I would claim that musical silence is not the void; and in effect it is also not only "cessation." Instead, it is "attenuation." Like reticence, or interrupted development, it expresses the wish to return to silence as soon as possible; an attenuation of intensity, it is at the threshold of the inaudible, a game played with almost-nothing.

So listen more closely! The pianissimo, though still audible, is the almost imperceptible form of the supersensory: it is *hardly* perceptible. On the border of the material and imma-

terial, of the physical and transphysical, the almost-nothing
designates minimal existence, beyond which would be nonexistence, nothing pure and simple.[18] The great masters of the
pianissimo, Fauré, Debussy, and Albeniz, operate at the limits
of noise and silence, in the border zone where those with
particularly sharp ears will perceive an infinitesimal sound,
micromusic. No hand is light enough, or so imponderable, that
it could extricate from the piano every infratone and ultratone
taken prisoner by Albeniz's divine *Jerez*. Archangelic hands
would be needed, and they would still be too heavy for this art
of brushing lightly, for an immaterial contact even more imperceptible than the phantom touch of the asymptote. At the end
of *Fête-Dieu à Seville*, music itself becomes a supernatural silence, a mysterious silence. Gabriel Fauré, the poet of half-light
and the penumbra (like Michelangelo or Maeterlinck) invites us
to speak softly, "very softly" (the last words of Verlaine's poem
"C'est l'extase" and the last words—almost—of *Pelléas et Mélisande*). "Let us delve into our love for deep silence," says "En
sourdine," one of Verlaine's *Fêtes galantes* in its whispering,
rustling night. Just as human beings keep watch for the "indistinct threshold where night becomes dawn"[19] and the moment
when day begins to darken, that they might witness the messages borne by dawn and twilight, so they listen, passionately,
for the birth and extinguishing of sound, that they might overhear the secrets harbored by life, and death. If the first and last
verses of Victor Hugo's *Djinns* correspond to the silences that
are anterior and ulterior limits of music, the second and pen-
ultimate verses represent two pianissimos, two minimal musics,
and not two nothings. They are the two almost-nothings, a
passage that represents nothing passing into something:

In the plain,
A sound is born;
This is the breath
Exhaled by night.

And then, something into nothing:

> This vague noise
> Lulled to its own sleep,
> It is the lament,
> (Almost extinguished)
> Of a saint
> For one who is dead.

Debussy for his part seeks to grasp the liminal moment when silence becomes music. This is the "antecedent pianissimo," music that is hardly audible, emerging from the "antecedent silence." In the opening of *La mer*, a clamor arises from the enigmatic depths where music is improvising itself into being. For the sea's silence is no more empty than the desert's: "Immense murmur, nonetheless silent," are the words of Charles van Leberghe, Fauré's favorite poet, from the "very first words" of the *Chanson d'Ève*.[20] All sorts of possible musics shudder within this undifferentiated rumor, the vibrating nebulousness that is inhabited by air's voice and water's voice, intermingled.

The other threshold gives access to terminal nothingness. Making infinite gradations in the nuances of imperceptibility, Debussy deliberately attenuates his decrescendos to the point where almost-nothing and nothing become indistinguishable. "Hardly," *estinto, perdendosi*. Music asymptotically approaches the extreme limit beyond which silence reigns: instrumental vibrations, dying away gradually, end by dying out into nothingness, like the lethal pianissimo that expires at the end of Gabriel Dupont's "La mort rôde," one of his "Lifeless Hours."[21] The beginning and end of Debussy's *Nocturne* for orchestra, "Nuages," is an immaterial tremor, sliding silence and shuddering plumes: archangel wings brushing featherbed clouds would make more noise than the violins' shivering bows, and threefold pianissimo "*ppp*," fourfold, a thousand-fold "*p*" or a hundred-thousand-fold "*p*" would convey no more than the

faintest idea of such an infinitesimal "piano." Mélisande, at
the end of act 5, dissolves into silence like the clouds of this
first *Nocturne*—cloud herself, a faint wind as she is the
"breath of night," impalpable, imponderable Mélisande is losing herself, and, thinned to nothingness, self-annihilating, she
will return to non-being.

The almost-nonexistent dies out at last as the whisper of its
own disappearance, *perdendosi*. The prelude Debussy called
"Brouillards" also annihilates itself as this same *perdendosi*, as
does the pointless gyration called "Mouvement"; in the same
way the piano prelude "Les fées sont des exquises danseuses"
fades away. The dying woman in act 5, no "exquisite dancer,"
is nonetheless veritable cloud and vapor: like the bubble that
bursts at the faintest touch, the "small, silent creature" disappears, conjured away by death. At the end of the second
movement of the *Faust Symphony*, the enthusiastic Faustian
theme, transfigured by Marguerite's passion, dies out in A-flat
major as a hyper-natural sonority, so sublime it seems to have
issued directly from the Beyond. Marguerite and Mélisande,
sisters in innocence. A simple sigh or (as Ivan Bunin says of
Olga Meshchorskaya, untimely dead) "a slight respiration":[22]
this is all that remains of Chaikovsky's *Berceuse* op. 72 once
sleep has ravished consciousness, and overwhelms it. The last
lines of Bunin's admirable story could surely be applied to
translucent Mélisande, "that slight hint of breath has now dis-
sipated into the All, in this cloud-covered sky, in the spring's
cold wind."

If silence smooths the way for the transmission of a "message," this is because the negation that is silence suppresses or
attenuates those aspects of experience that are most showy or
ostentatious. To seek silence is to seek a meta-empirical Beyond, a supersensory realm more essential by far than the
realm occupied by existence, which roars at high volume, with
a booming voice. This quest gets us ready—if not to recognize truth, then at least to receive it. The chimera of the Be-

yond will survive all disappointments. For the ancient Greeks, who were a visually oriented people, optical phenomenality was by far the more exuberant and attractive principle: thus, for them, the search for intelligible knowledge entailed the idea of converting the invisible into that which could be seen. For Heraclites, even the idea of super-sensible harmony involves the notion of an "invisible" harmony. Certainly the sixth book of the *Republic* insists upon the parallelism between vision and intuition: the myth of the cave beckons us to choose the path of light.

But this is allegory, and that is the point. Here and there within the visible thing—the sunlight—Plato begins to see the truth of the Good, a thing that can be known and that is more luminous than light itself. And if Platonic "contemplation" is always connected to the spectacular—that which can be envisaged—then ideas themselves are "forms" in a merely figural sense. In the *Banquet,* this notion explains the paradox of beauty as something beyond sensory and visual perception, supersensible and supervisible. Plotinus (in this, systematizing the "hyperbole") would envisage an "amorphous" and "nonplastic" hyperessence, existing beyond Appearance with its gaudy colors. Nevertheless, it would be an exaggeration to claim that the Greeks were not (in their own way) on the lookout for the inaudible mystery that lurks beyond acoustic appearances. Plato already senses the futility of rhetoric and flees the clamor of the agora. Is the dialectic of the dialogue— which cuts off discursive eloquence and fragments an orator's long tirade—not analogous to the "interrupted serenade," and in this, is it not one of the forms assumed by silence? Dialogue: is it not continuous discourse chopped off, and interrupted and fragmented? Irony, in turn, is a question asked in expectation of an answer, interrogation suspended in silence. Gorgias makes a peroration, but Socrates simply listens. This is perhaps the proper moment to recall that Satie, himself the author of a *Socrate,* gave his cadences the allure

of an "un-insistent request,"[23] and that Federico Mompou—
whose laconic style, whose reticence with regard to prolixity
and excess develops into a phobia—also nurtured a preference for the interrogative mode.

Walter Pater has reflected at some length upon Plato's admiration for the "apophthegma" and the ῥήματα βραχέα
(terse sentences) of the Lacedemonians.[24] Plato (master of the
dialogue, if not of aphorism) recognizes his own sobriety, his
own aversion toward verbal excess in these brief phrases; after
his fashion, he is applauding the repression of idle Athenian
conversation. In the works of the Neoplatonists, there is a
profound distrust of logos. Plotinus's *Of Contemplation*
pushes the paradox to its extreme in its search for the "word
that is mute," λόγος σιωπῶν.[25] From this point on, one no
longer even need ask a question; it is sufficient to be silent
and understand: ἐχρῆν μὲν μὴ ἐρωτᾶν, ἀλλὰ συνιέναι καὶ
αὐτὸν σιωπῇ, ὥσπερ ἐγὼ σιωπῶ καὶ οὐκ εἴθισμαι λέγειν,
"you ought not to ask, but to understand in silence, you, too,
just as I am silent and not in the habit of asking."[26] Not dar-
ing to offer even a single word, the wise man will soar into
God's presence once he has abandoned logos.[27] Pseudo-
Dionysius the Areopagite, who identifies invisible mystery and
inaudible mystery, thus points out a "shadow more luminous
than silence"[28] set apart from visible rays of light, for black
darkness is the origin of resplendent "light." Fyodor Ivanovich
Tyuchev writes, "thought becomes falsehood, once it is expressed."[29] This sense of the inexpressible, does it not seal the
lips of those who have felt it? The Bergsonian distrust of language will thus merge with the philosophy of the apophatic.

And hence it is not just that acoustic din—as an opaque
screen—puts obstacles in the way of truth and intercepts
communication. This din can be, in itself, a seductive, dia-
bolically deceptive principle, one that not only diverts but also
perverts. Odysseus, the allegorical personification of mystery,
covers his ears in order not to hear the Sirens, the principle of

Error—that is, to render himself deaf to suasive music as to treacherous temptation.

For the Siren's music is more than distracting noise, more than noise that diverts or dissipates, preventing reflective thought: it is a fraudulent art of pleasing. All that is really needed to stifle and obscure our silent dialogue with reason is the gaudy racket of the public market, ὁ ἐντὸς τῆς ψυχῆς πρὸς αὐτὴν διάλογος ἄνευ φωνῆς γιγόμενος, λόγος εἰρ-ημένος . . . σιγῇ πρὸς αὐτόν, "what we call thought is speech that occurs without the voice, inside the soul in conversation with itself . . . in silence to oneself."[30] But the Siren concert is not (just) gaudy racket. The enchantresses posted along the way to Ithaca—which is the road toward Truth—want to lead us astray, send us on a detour, and make us deviate from the narrow path. And just as light illuminates all presences, makes manifest the coexistence of existing things, and communicates being, yet can turn into deceptive shimmer in a mirage, thus the word, which can bring human beings together, can also isolate them from one another once it turns into a lie. The word, a double-edged sword, is a vehicle for intellectual activity yet also derails it, signifies and disfigures, bears meaning and prevents one from thinking at all.

But there is still more: of all forms of appearance, the form of appearance assumed by sound is the most futile: more so than space stirred by air, the Harlequin cape of our multi-colored existence, emptier than any hodgepodge of blaring, violently ostentatious color. Much (audible) ado about nothing! Optical appearance creates volume—though specious and inconsistent, appearing to be other and more than it is: yet at least the great bluff of existence will survive the instant, even if it deflates sooner or later. Even a ripple in the water extends beyond the instant. But acoustic furor's particular hollowness is futile twice over, demanding as it does continual renewal in order to endure. Failing that, it will fall flat and revert to silence. Thus, acoustic furor is actually the hollowness of hol-

lowness, *vanitas vanitatis*, futility to the second power. An
ephemeral mode, it demands constant maintenance. Sound
resounds in time, and collapses instantly if one does not
ceaselessly reanimate it, like the trumpet call that is broken off
when one no longer blows into the instrument. Must we
shout ourselves hoarse, till the end of time, that music might
endure?

Grandiloquent music, resembling angry shrieks, is a form
of emphatic stupidity: it sounds empty and it contains nothing but wind. If a frivolous definition of "emphasis" naively
mistakes sheer volume for reality, or takes appearance for essence, then appreciating understatement means coming to
terms with disproportion and makes us recognize that existence, with distracting irony, assumes paradoxical form, as a
chiasmus: there is no simple proportional relationship between a given being's true importance and the volume of
sound it emits, between its ontological weight and its phe-
nomenological acoustic volume. Any being's degree of Being
is not always in direct consequence to its phenomenal glare.
No, the most important thing is not necessarily that which
conveys the impression of importance. "His strength is astonishing to little children. He shifts an enormous stone (made of
pumice)."[31] Satie's humor, does it not serve to deflate the
megalomania inherent in glorious surface appearances? The
redundancy that wants to appear big as an ox is reduced to
the shady maneuver it always was.

More specifically, noise (which encumbers all space with its
presence) will have existence without a guarantee of consis-
tency or density. Truly important things make less noise than
loud, insolent existences, with all their fanfares. Understatement (not taken in by any of it) is thus the opposite of emphasis, just as seriousness is to futility. God, according to
scripture, does not come with the noise of wrathfulness but as
imperceptibly as a breeze. Or (not according to scripture, but
as I prefer to put it, to evoke *Pelléas et Mélisande* one more

time): God arrives on tiptoe, furtively, pianissimo, just like Death in act 5: an almost-nothing, an imperceptible sigh, softer, if possible, than Olga Meshchorskaya's breaths. Or, as Arkel says:

> I saw nothing. Are you sure? . . . I heard nothing at all . . . so quickly, so quickly . . . she departed without saying anything . . . she needs silence, now.

Many radical events and changes will resemble the deep, weary labor of Death in that they take place silently, in the clandestine realm of the almost-nothing. The work of thought makes no noise, nor more do lovers; they make no noise while absorbed in their mysterious, silent colloquy, and François de Sales pays homage to their taciturnity: "Even though lovers have nothing secret to say, they like nonetheless to say it secretly."[32]

Viewed in its positive aspects, silence provides a favorable condition for concentrated attention; as the *Phaedo* says, silence is the necessary condition for "contemplation." Not just blackness, but silence as well, is necessary for hearing the "interior voices" of reflection, which Malebranche dubbed "the Word of human intelligence." The author of *Méditations chrétiennes et metaphysiques* compared attention to a "natural prayer" that solicits grace from a super-sensory Truth. Human beings in a contemplative state can hear in silence, just as animals with night vision can see in the dark. Plotinus himself, who otherwise dismisses the noise made by logos, Plotinus seeks silence not to put a stethoscope to its chest and divine some inaudible language, supernatural speech, a secret voice, but to contemplate a great spectacle, θέαμα, θεώρημα.[33] It is in the Bible every so often that hearing trumps vision, and that God at certain moments reveals himself to man in the form of the spoken Word. Hear, O Israel! For while no one has ever seen God, some have been able to hear Him.[34]

Σκότος, γνόφος, φωνὴ μεγάλη, "gloom, darkness, a loud

voice," as Deuteronomy V.22 puts it. It is not from the midst of a cloud that God proclaims the Law?

It is silence that allows us to hear *another voice*, a voice speaking *another language*, a voice that comes *from elsewhere*. This unknown tongue spoken by an unknown voice, this *vox ignota*, hides behind silence just as silence itself lurks behind the superficial noise of daily existence. Knowledge deepened by dialectics enables an individual who listens attentively to burrow through thick layers of noise to discover transparent strata of silence. And then, he or she will delve into the infinite within the depths of silence, to discover therein the most secret of all musics. Silence is beyond noise, but the "invisible harmony" of the Greeks, the great cryptic or esoteric harmony, is beyond even silence itself. Imagine the look on the face of a man who had captured a barely perceptible message from some distant sphere: heart pounding, he would hold his breath, that all his senses might drink in the cryptogram, the unknown sign, the sigh that has come to him across infinite space.

In truth the "musical message" is no metaphysical message: or, at least, it is only metaphysical by virtue of a metaphor and, in some sense, spiritually. Music, this voice from another order, does *not* come from another world, and even less from the otherworldly. This distant voice is not in reality sent to us from far-off lands. Where does it come from, then, the unknown voice? From the conditions inside us, yet from nature exterior to us. Silence brings into being the latent counterpoint between past and future voices, a counterpoint that jams the noisy tumult of the present; and on the other hand, silence reveals the inaudible voice of absence, a voice that is concealing the deafening racket made by presences. Whereas music, audible silence, by nature seeks the pianissimo rustling of memory, heard like the voice of a distant friend who whispers at our mind's ear. I have shown how music, as the language of Becoming, will also be the language of memories, and how memory renders all expression evasive. Ricordanza, the spell of memory: furrowed by long silences, Franz Liszt's *Valses oubliées* appear out of the mists of memory. Debussy's prelude "Des pas sur la neige," a long meditation on the vestiges of departed presence, speaks (in a low voice) of the nostalgia of absence, of remorse and its melancholia. "Colloque sentimentale" evokes old things—things that are past, distant, irrevocable, things that will never again be—right before being collapsed into the nothingness of a frigid night. Confidences about things past are whispered into our mental ear.

But more than this: we also receive forecasts of things to come as well, and more still, things promised, hoped for, and things whose coming is passionately awaited. Rimsky-Korsakov's *Legend of the Invisible City of Kitezh* is telling us about the future: in that deep silence, in the midst of boundless solitude of the banks of the Volga, the soul's ear and the corporeal ear hear the distant bells; the distant sound takes shape not in the depths of reminiscence—in some mysterious past—but at the horizon of an undefined future. This is Celestial Kitezh: our hope. Lesser Kitezh is the real and perceptible city, as noisy as Musorgsky's open-air market in Limoges; and when its deafening racket falls silent, then and then alone do we hear the carillons of the invisible city. The city is invisible but not inaudible.

It is not just that silence allows memories of the past to be invoked, or the bells of Easters yet to come to be heard; silence also develops the infinitesimal sounds of a universal multipresence. Fyodor Tyuchev said it beautifully: just as night makes stars appear in the sky, so when the tumult that is vigilance withdraws, the sounds that are interior, the magical singing, the dream-like images of fantasy can appear. But night also unveils the secret noises of cosmic existence, and not just those of subjectively perceptible music. For night, as much as silence, discloses the infrasensory noise of nature to human consciousness. The innumerable voices that people midnight's silence will echo against the thunderous silence of noon. The susurrations of a nocturnal animal,[35] a falling dew-drop, the sigh of a blade of grass. It is late; from faraway a bell tolls the hours of the night; a fountain chatters beneath its breath in the darkness at the heart of the garden; the wind blows dead leaves and makes them crackle. "You could hear the water as it slept."[36] You could hear the grass as it grew. Just as you can hear something prowling somewhere at the edge of the moonlight, in act 4, scene 4 of *Pelléas et Mélisande*. Lend an ear to the vast rustlings of coleopteran wings, at the end of *L'Enfant et les Sortilèges*. In "The Night's Music," Bela Bartók listens to automatic insect chirping, even to the bird that taps its beak, repeatedly, on a hollow wooden tree trunk. And then—interrupting animal and vegetable sound—comes human singing, rising from faraway in the darkness.

Supersensory voices and infrasensory voices are something else entirely, of an entirely other sonic order than the noises of day. Just as clairvoyants, or those endowed with superhuman sight, see in the darkness—with second sight (which is intuition)—and see invisible essences hidden behind that which exists visibly, so silence allows a kind of "second hearing" to develop, aural finesse, which allows human beings to perceive the least murmur of wind and night. Silence is a good conductor: it transmits implications hidden within what we can and do hear and allows a universal mystery and its voices to approach human beings.

Music renews its strength at the fountain of silence. But in what sense? To appreciate this suitably, we must first learn to distrust optical metaphors and the specious symmetries of synaesthesia. For there is an entire rhetoric of silence that shares nothing with metaphysics, except its conceits. Is silence the night of words? Is night the silence of light? These are (self-evidently) manners of speaking. One easily attributes the quality of sound to silence since by means of contrasts silence makes sound appear, and sound divides silence, and disturbs silence. The "immense murmur" mentioned in the *Chansons d'Eve* is indistinguishable from the silence that has made it perceptible to begin with, and Gabriel Dupont writes a song about "the silence of water." Night noises, transcribed by Bartók: are they not the *noise of silence*?[37] And I myself: have I not talked about dialogue as a form of silence, the silence inherent in brachylogy? The idea of a deafening silence: would this not appear to be as perfectly aligned with the Areopagites' negative philosophy, as much as the paradox of a blinding darkness?

Above all, however, we need to resist a Manichaean urge to hypostatize silence. Not some least-of-Beings, not merely noise that is degraded or rarefied, not the primitive, negative state of a normally sonorous milieu (as is, for instance, the curse of losing one's voice)—silence is no longer the obverse of a positive. In its own way, it is a form of plenitude, in its own way, a vehicle that conveys other things: underneath the banal, busy plenitude of daily life, silence reveals a more dense, more inspiring plenitude, otherwise populated, inhabited by other voices: and thus, silence inverts the usual relationship between fullness and emptiness, just as understatement is not inexpressive, but allusive. In other words, just as the "inexpressive Espressivo" is not a lesser form of expressiveness, but a kind of eloquence, so silence is not Nonbeing, but, rather, something other than Being.

The other voice, the voice that silence allows us to hear, is named Music. Without being pointlessly metaphorical, one could nonetheless say that silence is the desert where music blossoms and that music, a desert flower, is itself a sort of enigmatic silence. Whether reminiscence or prophecy, music and the silence that envelops it are *of this world*. Yet if this enigmatic voice is not disclosing the secrets of the Beyond, it may nonetheless remind us of the mystery that *we* bear within ourselves. And if no one possesses physiological hearing acute enough to overhear messages from an otherworldly realm, everyone can hear this "romance" without words and without specific signifying powers, which is called music. Everyone understands the voice that takes us prisoner, and does so, moreover, where there is nothing to understand, no conclusion to be drawn—and yet the voice tells us of our fate. Isaiah said of solitude: it will flower like a lily, sprouting and growing everywhere; it will be in effusions of joy and praise; the glory of Lebanon will be granted it, the radiance of Mount Carmel and of Sharon. And what the prophet Isaiah says about solitude, I will in turn repeat about silence. Silence, too, will exult, and the roses of Sharon will blossom in its bare soil. The sands of silence will cover the tumultuous waters; the arid desert of silence will be peopled with murmurs and the sound of wings, with ineffable music. In solitude, where Fevronia once dwelled, as in the joyous din of daily life, we can sometimes hear the bells—the babble of bells from the City of Silence, which resound almost imperceptibly, in the depths of night.

Notes

THE *CHARME* OF JANKÉLÉVITCH

1. Originally published as "Lo *charme* di Jankélévitch," *Iride* 11 (Dec. 1998): 619–22. Translation by Maria Purciello.

2. *Music and the Ineffable;* see below, page 50.

3. Vladimir Jankélévitch, *La présence lointaine. Albeniz, Séverac, Mompou* (Paris: Éditions du Seuil, 1983), 157.

4. Federico Mompou's letter to Vladimir Jankélévitch, 21 July 1971, in *Intemporel. Bulletin de la Société Nationale de Musique,* no. 8 (October–December 1993): 10.

5. Vladimir Jankélévitch, *L'arte del sortilegio,* in *Manuel de Falla,* edited by Massimo Mila (Milan: Ricordi, 1962), 154.

6. *Music and the Ineffable;* see 149–50, below.

7. Vladimir Jankélévitch, *Le je-ne-sais-quoi et le presque-rien* (Paris: Seuil, 1980), 108.

8. Ibid. In *Music and the Ineffable,* he cites Henri Bremond as his source for the concept of *charme,* as well as the term itself. See 125, below.

9. *Music and the Ineffable;* see 106–7 below.

10. Ibid., see 102, below.

11. Ibid., see 89, below.

12. Ibid., see 87, below.

13. Jankélévitch, *Le je-ne-sais-quoi et le presque-rien,* 113.

14. Vladimir Jankélévitch, *Henri Bergson* (Paris: Presses universitaires de France, 1989), 275.

15. Vladimir Jankélévitch, *De l'amour,* in Françoise Schwab, ed., *Premiéres et derniéres pages* (Paris: Éditions du Seuil, 1994), 247.

16. Jankélévitch, *Le je-ne-sais-quoi et le presque-rien,* 111–12.

17. Ibid., 113.

18. Vladimir Jankélévitch, *Préface* to Philippe-Fauré-Fremiet, *Esquisse d'une philosophie concrète* (Paris: Presses universitaires de France, 1954), xi.

19. Jankélévitch, *La présence lointaine*, 158.

20. Jankélévitch, *L'arte del sortilegio*, 154–55.

21. Vladimir Jankélévitch, *De l'ipséité*, in *Premières et dernières pages*, 183.

22. Manuel de Falla, *El amor brujo, Orquestra de Cambra Teatre Lliure, con Ginesa Ortega*, "Harmonia mundi" 945219.

23. *Music and the Ineffable*, see 129, below.

24. As he puts it in *Music and the Ineffable* (see 83, below):

> With this Charm (the musical act), there is nothing to 'think' about, or—*and this amounts to the same*—there is food for thought, in some form, for all infinity; the Charm engenders speculation inexhaustibly, is inexhaustible as the fertile ground for perplexity, and the same Charm is born of love. Infinite speculation, as soon as it becomes exhilaration pure and simple, is analogous to the poetic state.

25. Jankélévitch, *Pelléas et Pénélope*, in *Premières at dernières pages*, 265.

JANKÉLÉVITCH'S SINGULARITY

1. *Maurice Ravel* (Paris: Éditions Rieder, 1939). Revised as *Ravel* (Paris: Seuil, 1956; followed by numerous reprintings, and a new, expanded edition, ed. Jean-Michel Nectoux, 1995). Translated into English by Margaret Crosland (New York: Grove Press, 1959; reprinted by Greenwood Press, 1976).

2. See *L'odyssée de la conscience dans la dernière philosophie de Schelling* (Paris; F. Alcan, 1932); *La mauvaise conscience: Valeur et signification de la mauvaise conscience* (Paris: F. Alcan, 1933; second edition, Paris: PUF, 1951; republished Paris: Aubier-Montaigne, 1966 and 1981); *Bergson* (Paris: F. Alcan, 1931) revised as *Henri Bergson* (first edition, Paris: PUF, 1959; second edition, Paris: PUF, 1975; reprinted, Paris: PUF, 1989). A complete bibliography of Jankélévitch's work, including his numerous articles, appears in *Premières et dernières pages*.

3. Ida Jankélévitch, with Marcelle Meyer, premiered Milhaud's two-piano piece *Scaramouche* in 1937. She was also an acquaintance of Rilke, who dedicated his poem "La Porteuse des Fleurs" (1924) jointly to her and her husband, the poet Jean Cassou, who would become famous as a prominent leader in the Résistance during World War II.

4. *Gabriel Fauré et ses mélodies* (Paris: Plon, 1938). This was revised as *Gabriel Fauré: ses mélodies, son esthétique* (Paris: Plon, 1951),
then expanded into *Fauré et l'inexprimable* (Paris: Plon, 1974). His
pre-war articles include "Franz Liszt et les étapes de la musique moderne," *Musique* (1929): 701–6, 898–907; "Le symbolisme et la musique: Satie le simulateur," *Europe* 162 (1936): 249–56 (incorporated
into the Satie chapters in *Le Nocturne* 1957, [see note 5 below] and in
La musique et les heures [Paris: Seuil, 1988]); "Le nocturne," *Cahiers
du sud* (Special Number, 1937): 73–78 (incorporated into *Le Nocturne* 1942 [see note 5 below], *Le Nocturne* 1957, and *La musique et
les heures* 1988]; and "La sérénade interrompue," in *La Revue musicale* 19 (December 1938): 40–50 (incorporated into *Ravel* 1939 and
Ravel 1956; see note 1 above).

5. *Le nocturne* (Lyon: Marius Audin, 1942). This was a limited
edition of one thousand copies; the book was later reprinted and
expanded (Paris: Albin Michel, 1957) and reprinted in part as one
section in *La musique et les heures* (see note 4 above).

6. See Davidson, "Introductory Remarks," 545. Catherine Clément discusses Jankélévitch in "Au rhapsode," in Monique Basset, ed.,
Écrit pour Vladimir Jankélévitch (Paris: Flammarion, 1978), 31–47;
and in "Through Voices, History," in Mary Ann Smart, ed., *Siren
Songs* (Princeton: Princeton University Press, 2000), 24; he also appears as a fictional character ("Janké") in her novel *La Putain du
diable* (Paris: Flammarion, 1996).

7. Roland Barthes, "Musica Practica," in *The Responsibility of
Forms*, trans. Richard Howard (Berkeley: University of California
Press, 1985), 261–66. Clément has written of Jankélévitch's and Barthes' "shared theoretical sensuality" despite their very different per-
sonae and personal lives; see "Le Messager du Printemps," *Magazine
littéraire* 333 (June 1995): 24–27, especially 24.

8. See 77, 78–79, below.

9. His preface to Stefan Jarocinski's book *Debussy, Impressionism
and Symbolism* (London: Eulenberg, 1976) was translated by Rollo
Myers; an essay on Bergson appeared in an English-language col-
lected volume, *The Bergsonian Heritage*, ed. Thomas Hanna (Columbia: Columbia University Press, 1962).

10. "Should We Pardon Them?" trans. Ann Hobart, *Critical Inquiry* 22 (spring 1996): 552–72; see also "Do Not Listen to What
They Say, Look at What They Do," trans. Ann Hobart, *Critical Inquiry* 22 (spring 1996): 549–51. Davidson's "Introductory Remarks"
were written to put these two essays, and their author, in context for
Anglophone readers; see also Arnold Davidson and Nancy R. Kne-
zevic, trans., "Pelléas and Pénélope," *Critical Inquiry* 26 (spring
2000): 584–90. Jankélévitch's moral philosophy, described as "a dis-

course left behind by a hero of the French Resistance," was the subject of a *New Yorker* article in 1994, Paul Berman's "Reflections: The Other and the Almost the Same," *The New Yorker* (February 28, 1994): 61–66.

11. Davidson, "Introductory Remarks," 546–47.

12. This point is made by Davidson; see xii, above.

13. See 89, below.

PREFACE

1. Letter of 29 August 1903, Gabriel Fauré, *Lettres intimes*, ed. Philippe Fauré-Fremiet (Paris: La Colombe, 1951), 78.

CHAPTER 1
THE "ETHICS" AND THE "METAPHYSICS" OF MUSIC

1. *Republic* III, 401d.

2. *La musique*, rev. ed. (Paris: J. Pinasseau, 1928).

3. *Laws* VII, 800e:

Just as a corpse is escorted with Carian music by hired mourners. Such music would also form the fitting accompaniment for hymns of this kind; and the garb befitting these funeral hymns would not be any crowns nor gilded ornaments, but just the opposite, for I want to get done with this subject as soon as I can. Only I would have us ask ourselves again this single question: are we satisfied to lay this down as our first typical rule for hymns?

4. *Republic* III, 398d–e.

5. *Republic* III: 399c,d; as translated by G.M.A. Grube, in J. Cooper, ed., *Plato: Complete Works* (Indianapolis: Hackett, 1997). See also *Laws* VII, 812d: "The multiple strings designed to let all harmonies be heard."

6. See *Republic* III, 411b, σίδηρον ἐμάλαξεν, "iron is softened."

7. *The Wanderer and His Shadow* in *Human, All Too Human* II, aphorism 167.

8. Reported by Maxim Gorky, *Trois Russes*, trans. Dumesnil de Gramont (Paris: Gallimard, 1935), 12. Cf. Paul Boyer, *Chex Tolstoi: Entreties à Iasnaïa Polana* (Bibliothèque russe de l'Institut d'Études slaves, 1950), 53. On Tolstoy's relationships to music: Romain Rolland, *Vie de Tolstoi* (Paris: Hachette, 1928), 140–46.

9. Plotinus, *Enneads*, trans. A. H. Armstrong (Cambridge, Mass.: Harvard University Press, 1988), V.8, 1.

10. Plato, *Symposium*, 215c.

11. See Gisèle Brelet's important work, *Le Temps musicale* (Paris: PUF, 1949), vol. 1.

CHAPTER 2
THE INEXPRESSIVE "ESPRESSIVO"

1. Trans. note: "La sérénade interrompue" is one of Jankélévitch's favorite images, referring specifically to Debussy piano prelude but more generally to the aesthetic pathos as well as the ethical dimension of a musical gesture that represents a cutting-off or even a self-disciplined refusal of Romantic music making. One of his earliest articles, an essay on Ravel written in 1938, bears this name.

2. See also Ravel, *Ma mère l'oye*, Tableau 3; César Franck, *Variations symphoniques*, rehearsal nos. E and F; Bartók, *Nine Little Piano Pieces* (1926); Turina, *Duo sentimental* ("Miniatures," VI).

3. Maurice Ravel, *Ma mère l'oye*, Tableau 3.

4. Only Georges Migot, perhaps, aims to give the dialogue of the piano and the violin, or of the piano and the cello, a sense that distinguishes it from the sonata.

5. Fauré, *Dolly* op. 56, no. 5; Bizet, *Jeux d'enfants*, op. 22, no. 11; Smetana, *Ženich a nevěsta* (*The Couple*).

6. Hugo Wolf, *Mörike-Lieder* III, no. 35, "Frage und Antwort"; Bartók, *Mikrokosmos* I, 14. Cf. also II, 65 ("Dialogue"), and III, 88 ("Duo pour chalumeaux").

7. J. Chantavoine, *Beethoven* (Paris: Alcan, 1913), 163.

8. See Roland-Manuel, *Sonate, que me veux-tu?* (Lausanne: Mermod, 1957), 112, on the "thematics of return:" he insists vehemently on the circularity of musical time.

9. Bremond, *Prière et poésie* (Paris: B. Grasset, 1926), 10–11 (apropos Cardinal Newman); see also the citation from the Abbé Dubos, 11.

10. Trans. note: this refers to the "Scottish philosophy" of common sense, associated with such eighteenth-century philosophers as Reid, Stewart, Mackintosh, et al., who were dissenters from Locke's doctrine of ideas and Berkeley's idealism, as from skepticism in general.

11. Stravinsky, *Chroniques de ma vie* (Paris: Denoël et Steele, 1935), vol. 1, 14.

12. *Essai sur les données immédiates de la conscience* (Paris: Alcan, 1911), 120–21.

13. Bergson, *Deux sources de la morale et de la religion* (Paris: Alcan, 1932), 51, *La pensée et le mouvement* (Paris: Alcan, 1934), 160.

14. Aristotle, *Nichomechaean Ethics* II. 1.

15. *Chroniques de ma vie*, vol. 1, 116 (also see 158). See also vol. 2, 160–61; and *Poétique musical* (Paris: Éditions le Bon Plaisir, 1952),

116; Roland-Manuel, *Sonate, que me veux-tu?* and Alain, *Prélimi-naires à l'Esthétique* (Paris: Gallimard, 1939), 230. Only Paul Dukas sometimes takes the opposite tack: *Les Écrits de Paul Dukas sur la musique* (Paris: S.E.F., 1948), 123.

16. Trans. note: Schubert's *and* Rachmaninoff's short piano pieces, *Moments musicales.*

17. Trans. note: Debussy's prelude "Broulliards."

18. Trans. note: Jankélévitch uses the distinction between *réalisme*, which aspires to objectivity, and *vérisme*, which strives for an emotional truth, a realism of the passions.

19. Letter to Stasov, 7 (19) August 1875.

20. In 1916–17, while residing in the vicinity of Petrograd, Prokofiev had read Kant and Schopenhauer.

21. See Saint-Saens' *Carnival of the Animals.*

22. Villa-Lobos, *Os bichinos.*

23. Trans. note: "Jeu de vagues" is the second movement of *La Mer*; "Jeux d'eau" refers to Ravel's piano piece, the "fountain" that plays in a human garden.

24. *Mikrokosmos* VI, 142; see also V, 132, and VI, 144; cf. V, 135, and IV, 107; *Out of Doors* no. 4; and Prokofiev op. 65, no. 8.

25. Liszt composed this piece in 1881, and it was published for the first time in 1927.

26. *Écrits sur la musique*, 532.

27. Jean Cassou, *Le Janus ou de la Création* (Paris: Caractères, 1957), 11–13; ibid., *Trois poètes* (Paris: Plon, 1954), 31, 34, 35 (on Rilke): "The soul will create a face for itself" ["l'âme se fera visage"].

28. See his second *Chanson madécasse, L'Enfant et les sortilèges* (the animals' cry when they attack the Child); *Daphnis et Chloé* (the wordless "cries" of the warriors).

29. Eric Satie, *Cinq Grimaces pour le "Songe d'une nuit d'été."*

30. Trans. note: The terms refer to the two conventional "moods" or subsections in Liszt's Hungarian dances, the fast finale versus the slow and melancholy opening section.

31. See Raymond Bayer, *Léonard de Vinci: la grâce* (Paris: Alcan, 1933), 199–221.

32. See Bartók, *Nine Little Piano Pieces*, no. 7.

33. See *Poème satanique* op. 36; *Étrangeté* op. 63.

34. Prokofiev: op. 12, no. 9; op.17 (*Sarcasmes*); op. 22, no. 10; op. 3, no. 2. See also *Choute*, op. 21. Alexandre Tansman, *Onze Inter-ludes*, no. 2; *Cinq impressions*, no. 2. Karol Szymanowski, *Masques* op. 34, no. 2: *Tantris le Bouffon.* Bartók, *Mikrokosmos* V, 130 ("Burlesque rustique"), and 139 ("Bouffon"), and *Three Burlesques* op. 8.

35. Trans. note: A quotation from Verlaine's poem "Mandoline" (from *Fêtes galantes*), set by both Fauré and Debussy as a song.

36. Federico Mompou, *Suburbis*, 2. Darius Milhaud, *Ipanema* (*Sandades do Brazil* I, 5).

37. Rabindranath Tagore, *The Gardener*, no. 41.

38. *En vacances* I, 3.

39. *Phaedo* 117, d–e: "And we, hearing him, we were ashamed and held back our tears."

40. Van Lerberghe, "En un pénombre," *Le jardin clos*, no. 6; see Verlaine's *En sourdine*.

41. Darius Milhaud, *Leme* (end) (*Saudades* I, 3); Poulenc, *Sonata for Violin and Piano*, II (end).

42. Op. 40, no. 12.

43. *Écrits sur la musique*, 532.

44. Also a work by Roussel.

45. Liszt, *Études transcendentes* no. 9, *Arbre de Noël* (*Weihnachtsbaum*) no. 10 ("Jadis"), *Le mal du pays*. Chaikovsky, *Souvenir de Gaspal* op. 2, *Souvenir d'un lieu cher* op. 42, *Souvenir de Florence* op. 70; *Passé lointain* op. 72, no. 17. Arensky, *Ne m'oubliez pas* op. 36, no. 10. Albeniz, *Espagne-Souvenirs*. Roger Ducasse, *Souvenance*. Vítězslav Novák, *Vzpomínky* op. 6. Suk, *Vzpomínání* op. 28, no. 5. Nikolay Myaskovsky, *Videniya* op. 21, no. 1. Anatoly Lyadov, *Vospominaniye* op. 64, no. 4. Guy Ropartz, *Musiques au jardin*, "Les vieux souvenirs surgissent de l'ombre." Dvořák, *Vzpomínání* op. 85.

46. Plotinus, *Enneads*, VI. 7, 22; I.24.

47. After Bürger's Ballad; see also Richard Strauss's *Enoch Arden*, based on the poem by Tennyson.

48. Op. 20, 25, 31 nos. 3, 34, 35, 42, 48, 51. By Prokofiev, op. 3, 12 (*Légende*), 31 (*Contes de la vieille Grand-mère*). Myaskovsky, *Sonata* op. 84; see also op. 74 (*Improvisations*). Lyapunov, op. 59. Dvořák, op. 59.

49. Souriau, *L'abstraction sentimentale* (Paris: Hachette, 1925); R. Bayer, *Traité d'Esthétique* (Paris: A. Colin, 1956), 71.

50. Fauré, *Pièces brèves* op. 84, no. 7; *Dolly* op. 56, no. 5 (cf. op. 6, no. 2).

51. Scriabin op. 57, no. 1; Myaskovsky op. 29 (*Vospominaniya*, no. 3, "Désespoir"). Anatoly Lyadov, *La Douleur* op. 17, no. 1; *Tentation*, op. 64; op. 1, "Iz slyoz moikh" ("From My Tears") (for piano and voice). Anatoly Alexandrov, *Visions*, no. 4.

52. See Pierre Lasserre, *Les idées de Nietzsche sur la musique* (Paris: Payot, 1907), 65–66. See also Nietzsche, *Werke* IX, 218–20.

53. Alexandrov, *Videniya* op. 21 (1919–23); Myaskovsky, *Vospominaniya* op. 29.

54. *Horizons sonores* (Paris: Flammarion, 1956).

55. *Sonate, que me veux-tu?* vol. 2.

56. Debussy (*Nocturnes for Orchestra*); Roussel (op. 22); Albeniz;

(*Iberia* I, no. 3); Rimsky-Korsakov, *Svetlïy prazdnik* (*Russian Easter Festival*), Liszt, etc.

57. Jean Cassou, *Trois poètes*, 69 (concerning Milosz).

58. Cited by Siohan, "Possibilités et limites de l'abstraction musicale" *Journal de Psychologie* (1959): 258. See also Maurice Emmanuel, *Pelléas et Mélisande de Debussy* (Paris: Éditions Mellotée, 1950), 35.

59. *Sur un sentier ombragé*, VI.

60. Heinrich Heine, cited by Chaikovsky, in a letter to Madame von Meck, concerning Symphony no. 6.

61. Fauré, *Lettres intimes*, 131–32. See also Philippe Fauré-Fremiet, *Gabriel Fauré* (Paris: A. Michel, 1957), 28, 156.

CHAPTER 3
THE CHARM AND THE ALIBI

1. Stravinsky, *Poétique musicale*, 8–9. See also Jean Cassou, *Situation de l'art moderne* (Paris: Éditions de Minuit, 1950), 38.

2. *Phaedo*, 60e.

3. Philippe Fauré-Fremiet, *Pensée et récréation* (Paris: Alcan, 1934), II and VII. See also Gisèle Brelet, *L'interprétation créatrice* (Paris: PUF, 1951).

4. *Prière et poésie*, xii.

5. Unpublished letter from Fauré to his son Philippe, on the subject of *Caligula*'s "Air de Danse."

6. *Enneads* VI.8, 11.

7. At the end of *The Death of Ivan Ilytch*.

8. Jean Cassou, *La Rose et le Vin*, commentary (Paris: Caractères, 1952).

9. See the end of Tolstoy's *Resurrection*; as well as Part V of his *The Kingdom of God Is within You*.

10. "Do not pretend": see Alain, *Préliminaires à l'Esthetique*, 203.

11. As Bergson says in *Les deux sources de la morale et de la religion*.

12. *Variété* V, 138.

13. *Zur Geschichte der neueren Philosophie*, *Werke* vol. 10 (Stuttgart: J. G. Cotta, 1859), 100–101.

14. Cited by Tolstoy, according to Maxim Gorky, *Trois Russes*, 16.

15. Étienne Souriau explored this question at length in *La Correspondance des arts* (Paris: Flammarion, 1947).

16. *Mikrokosmos* II, 64: "Line against Point."

17. *Horizons sonores*, 113–14, 116.

18. This is demonstrated by one of Charles Bordes's songs, "Le son du coeur s'afflige vers les bois."

19. Satie writes, "So as to make a cross" between the staves of his third *Gnossienne*: but, it is clear that this has to do with the position he forces the right hand to assume on the keys. See N. Cherbachov, op. 8.

20. Turina: *Caminando, Album de Viaje, Viaje maritimo,* etc. Prokofiev, op. 59: *Progulka.* Musorgsky: *Pictures at an Exhibition.*

21. Liszt: *Sposalizion, Il Penseroso, Bataille des Huns,* etc; and Musorgsky, *Pictures at an Exhibition.* See also Zdenek Fibich, *Malířské Studie* op. 56 (after Ruysdaël, Brueghel, Corrège, Watteau, Fra Giovanni da Fiesole).

22. Chaikovsky, *Eugene Onegin,* act 2, scene 2. Pushkin, VI, 21.

23. "Bypasses": this is said by Stravinsky, *Chroniques de ma vie,* vol. 2, 162.

24. *Ibid.,* vol. 1, 158.

25. This is the subtitle he gave to his operas *Guercoeur* and *Bérénice*

26. *Delphic Paean* I.6.

27. *Bible de l'Humanité,* 204–205.

28. See *Phaedrus* 229b; Satie's *Socrate* II (vocal score p. 22).

29. Henri Bremond, *La poésie pure* (Paris: Grasset, 1926), 21, 24.

30. Jean Cassou, *Situation de l'Art moderne,* 98–99.

31. Georges Migot, *Lexique,* article "Monody."

32. See *Mikrokosmos* 18–21, 52, 77, 104, 108, 112, 116, 137.

33. Gervais, *Étude comparée des langages harmoniques de Fauré et de Debussy* (Diss., Univ. de Paris, Sorbonne, 1954), 13, 152.

34. In the second string quartet op. 45 (first movement): in C, and then in "J."

35. Gabriel Fauré, *Lettres intimes,* 142 (letter of 12 August 1907); see also Fauré-Fremiet, *Gabriel Fauré,* 150–51, on the tempo of the second Impromptu.

36. See the end of Debussy's preludes "Danseuses de Delphes," and "Les Collines d'Anacapri," *Masques,* "Les Cloches à travers les feuilles," from *Images* for piano. See also Bartók's *Dance Suite,* IV; Albeniz, "El Polo" from *Iberia,* and the end of "L'Été" (from *Les Saisons*); Balakirev's *Au Jardin.*

37. See measures 50 and 52, 93 and 96.

38. Serge Rachmaninoff, op. 16

39. Plato, *Laws,* VII, 802d: βελτίους (better).

40. Trans. note: the section title refers to the Latin proverb, "Musica Laetitiae Comes Medicina Dolorum"—"Music is the companion of joy and the medicine of sorrow." This proverb is inscribed on the lid of the virginal in Vermeer's famous painting *The Music Lesson,* as Jankélévitch notes at the end of the section.

41. Aristotle, *Politics,* trans. C.D.C. Reeve (Indianapolis: Hackett, 1998), VIII, 1337b.

42. Aristotle, *Politics,* VIII, 1342a.

CHAPTER 4
MUSIC AND SILENCE

1. *Soirs amoricains* op. 21, no 1: "Au large des clochers"
2. Jean Cassou, *Trois poètes*, 73, 110, silence is the "cradle of music."
3. See Aldous Huxley's essay "Music at Night."
4. Borodin: his essence.
5. Musorgsky, *Bïdlo* (from *Pictures at an Exhibition*).
6. Musorgsky, *Il vecchio castello* (ibid.), Bartók, *Pro dêti* (*For Children*, no. 42); Debussy "Fêtes," from the *Nocturnes for Orchestra*.
7. "One doubts—the night—I hear—everything flees—everything passes—in space—effacing—all noise." See Alain's commentary, *Préliminaires à l'esthétique*, 271.
8. Ravel, *Histoires naturelles*, "Le Grillon." See also *Pelléas et Mélisande*, act 2, scene 1.
9. Rachmaninoff, *Ostrovok* op. 14. Chabrier, *L'île heureuse*. Debussy, *L'île joyeuse*.
10. See *May Night* act 3; *The Legend of the Invisible City of Kitezh* act 3 scene 3; *Snegurochka* act 4; *Mlada* acts 2 and 4; *Sadko* act 2.
11. Aristotle, *Physics*, 221b.
12. *Phaedrus* 242a.
13. In "Sainte," set to music by Ravel.
14. *Enneads* VI.8, 19.
15. *Enneads* VI.8, 19.
16. *Pelléas*, act 5, scene 2.
17. *Enneads* VI.8, 11.
18. Almost-nothings: Debussy, the end of *Pelléas* act 1; "Les Cloches à travers les feuilles" from the *Images* for piano; *Mouvement* for piano; the end of *Jeux*; the end of "Brouillards." Nothing more: Debussy, the end of *Lindaraja* for two pianos; the end of "Le Faune" (*Fêtes galantes* II); the end of "Colloque sentimental"; "De grève" from *Proses lyriques*.
19. Fauré, *Le Jardin clos*, op. 106, no. 3: "La Messagère."
20. Gabriel Fauré, *La chanson d'Ève* op. 95, 1: "Paradise" (the title was invented by Fauré).
21. *Heures dolantes* XI.
22. In his *Un légère respiration* (1916). And "Wie ein Hauch" (Schoenberg, *Sechs kleine Klavierstücke* op. 19, no. 6 [end]); Debussy, "Colloque sentimental," (end); Liszt, *Faust Symphony* movement 2.
23. See *Le Fils des Étoiles*, the first *Gnossienne*. Also, Mompou, *1er Dialogue*, *Scènes d'enfants* ("Jeu").
24. See Plato, *Protagoras* 342e, 343a. See Pater, *Platon et le Platonisme*, trans. Samuel Jankélévitch (Paris: Payot, 1923), 235–36; 264.

25. *Enneads* III.8, 6; "silent rational form" in Armstrong's translation.

26. *Enneads* III.8, 4; see also VI.8, 11.

27. *Enneads* IV.8, 19.

28. *Mystical Theology*, 997b.

29. "Silentium" (1830). See Fyodor Stepun, *La tragédie de la création* (Paris: Logos russe, 1910); *La tragédie de la conscience mystique* (Paris: Logos russe, 1911–12). Also S. L. Frank, *Zivoye znaniye* (Berlin: Obelisk, 1923).

30. Plato, *The Sophist* 263e, trans. N. P. White, in J. Cooper, ed., *Plato: Complete Works* (Hackett, London: 1997); Plato, *Theaetetus* 190a; see also *Philebus* 38e.

31. Satie, *Le porteur de grosses pierres* (*Chapitres tournés en tous sens*, 2).

32. *Traité de l'amour de Dieu* VI: 6.

33. *Enneads* III.8, 4; and VI.8, 19 θεάσεται (he will see); ιδών (seeing).

34. Θεὸν οὐδεὶς ἑώρακεν πώποτε (*John* I.18, no one has ever seen God); θεὸν οὐδεὶς πώποτε τεθέαται (*I Ep. John* IV.12, no one has even seen God); οὔτε φωνὴν αὐτοῦ πώποτε ἀκηκόατε οὔτε εἶδος αὐτοῦ ἑωράκατε (*John* V.37, you have never heard his voice, not have you seen his form); see also Exodus XXXIII.20; Deuteronomy V. 22.

35. Bartók, *Microcosmos* II: 63 "Susurration."

36. *Pelléas et Mélisande* act 2, scene 1.

37. *Pelléas et Mélisande* act 2, scene 3.

Index of Names